LINQ
Pocket Reference

LINQ
Pocket Reference

Joseph Albahari and Ben Albahari

O'REILLY®

Beijing · Cambridge · Farnham · Köln · Paris · Sebastopol · Taipei · Tokyo

LINQ Pocket Reference

by Joseph Albahari and Ben Albahari

Copyright © 2008 Joseph Albahari and Ben Albahari. All rights reserved. Printed in Canada.

Published by O'Reilly Media, Inc., 1005 Gravenstein Highway North, Sebastopol, CA 95472.

O'Reilly books may be purchased for educational, business, or sales promotional use. Online editions are also available for most titles (*safari.oreilly.com*). For more information, contact our corporate/institutional sales department: (800) 998-9938 or *corporate@oreilly.com*.

Editor: Laurel R.T. Ruma

Production Editor: Loranah Dimant

Proofreader: Loranah Dimant

Indexer: Julie Hawks

Cover Designer: Karen Montgomery

Interior Designer: David Futato

Illustrator: Robert Romano

Printing History:

February 2008:   First Edition.

ISBN: 978-0-596-51924-7

[TM]

Contents

Getting Started — 1

Lambda Queries — 4
  Chaining Query Operators — 4
  Composing Lambda Expressions — 6
  Natural Ordering — 9
  Other Operators — 9

Comprehension Queries — 10
  Iteration Variables — 12
  Query Syntax Versus SQL Syntax — 13
  Query Syntax Versus Lambda Syntax — 13
  Mixed Syntax Queries — 14

Deferred Execution — 15
  Reevaluation — 16
  Outer Variables — 17
  How Deferred Execution Works — 17
  Chaining Decorators — 19
  How Queries Are Executed — 20

Subqueries — 22
  Subqueries and Deferred Execution — 25

Composition Strategies   **25**
    Progressive Query Building   25
    The into Keyword   27
    Wrapping Queries   28

Projection Strategies   **30**
    Object Initializers   30
    Anonymous Types   30
    The let Keyword   32

Interpreted Queries   **33**
    How Interpreted Queries Work   35
    AsEnumerable   38

LINQ to SQL   **40**
    LINQ to SQL Entity Classes   40
    DataContext   42
    Automatic Entity Generation   45
    Associations   45
    Deferred Execution with LINQ to SQL   47
    DataLoadOptions   48
    Updates   50

Building Query Expressions   **52**
    Delegates Versus Expression Trees   53
    Expression Trees   55

Query Operator Overview   **59**

Filtering   **62**
    Where   63
    Take and Skip   65
    TakeWhile and SkipWhile   65
    Distinct   66

Projecting 66
    Select 67
    SelectMany 72

Joining 82
    Join and GroupJoin 83

Ordering 92
    OrderBy, OrderByDescending, ThenBy, ThenByDescending 92

Grouping 95
    GroupBy 96

Set Operators 100
    Concat and Union 100
    Intersect and Except 100

Conversion Methods 101
    OfType and Cast 101
    ToArray, ToList, ToDictionary, ToLookup 103
    AsEnumerable and AsQueryable 104

Element Operators 104
    First, Last, Single 105
    ElementAt 106
    DefaultIfEmpty 107

Aggregation Methods 107
    Count and LongCount 107
    Min and Max 108
    Sum and Average 109
    Aggregate 110

Quantifiers 111
    Contains and Any 111
    All and SequenceEqual 112

Generation Methods   **112**
    Empty   112
    Range and Repeat   113

LINQ to XML   **113**
    Architectural Overview   114

X-DOM Overview   **115**
    Loading and Parsing   117
    Saving and Serializing   118

Instantiating an X-DOM   **118**
    Functional Construction   119
    Specifying Content   120
    Automatic Deep Cloning   121

Navigating/Querying an X-DOM   **122**
    Child Node Navigation   122
    Parent Navigation   126
    Peer Node Navigation   127
    Attribute Navigation   128

Updating an X-DOM   **128**
    Simple Value Updates   128
    Updating Child Nodes and Attributes   129
    Updating Through the Parent   130

Working with Values   **133**
    Setting Values   133
    Getting Values   133
    Values and Mixed Content Nodes   135
    Automatic XText Concatenation   136

Documents and Declarations   **136**
     XDocument   136
     XML Declarations   139

Names and Namespaces   **140**
     Specifying Namespaces in the X-DOM   142
     The X-DOM and Default Namespaces   143
     Prefixes   145

Projecting into an X-DOM   **147**
     Eliminating Empty Elements   149
     Streaming a Projection   150
     Transforming an X-DOM   151

Index   **153**

LINQ Pocket Reference

LINQ, or Language Integrated Query, allows you to write structured type-safe queries over local object collections and remote data sources. It is a new feature of C# 3.0 and .NET Framework 3.5.

LINQ lets you query any collection implementing IEnumerable<>, whether an array, list, XML DOM, or remote data source (such as a table in SQL Server). LINQ offers the benefits of both compile-time type checking and dynamic query composition.

The core types that support LINQ are defined in the System.Linq and System.Linq.Expressions namespaces in the System.Core assembly.

NOTE

The examples in this book mirror the examples in Chapters 8–10 of *C# 3.0 in a Nutshell* (O'Reilly) and are preloaded into an interactive querying tool called LINQPad. You can download LINQPad from *http://www.linqpad.net/*.

Getting Started

The basic units of data in LINQ are *sequences* and *elements*. A sequence is any object that implements the generic IEnumerable interface, and an element is each item in the sequence. In the following example, names is a sequence, and Tom, Dick, and Harry are elements:

```
string[] names = { "Tom", "Dick", "Harry" };
```

We call such a sequence a *local sequence* because it represents a local collection of objects in memory.

A *query operator* is a method that transforms a sequence. A typical query operator accepts an *input sequence* and emits a transformed *output sequence*. In the Enumerable class in System.Linq, there are around 40 query operators, all implemented as static extension methods, called *standard query operators*.

NOTE

LINQ also supports sequences that can be dynamically fed from a remote data source such as a SQL Server. These sequences additionally implement the IQueryable<> interface and are supported through a matching set of standard query operators in the Queryable class. For more information, see the upcoming "Interpreted Queries" section.

A *query* is an expression that transforms sequences with query operators. The simplest query comprises one input sequence and one operator. For instance, we can apply the Where operator on a simple array to extract those whose length is at least four characters as follows:

```
string[] names = { "Tom", "Dick", "Harry" };

IEnumerable<string> filteredNames =
  System.Linq.Enumerable.Where (
    names, n => n.Length >= 4);

foreach (string n in filteredNames)
  Console.Write (n + "|");           // Dick|Harry|
```

Because the standard query operators are implemented as extension methods, we can call Where directly on names—as though it were an instance method:

```
IEnumerable<string> filteredNames =
  names.Where (n => n.Length >= 4);
```

For this to compile, you must import the System.Linq namespace. Here's a complete example:

```
using System;
using System.Linq;

class LinqDemo
{
  static void Main()
  {
    string[] names = { "Tom", "Dick", "Harry" };
    IEnumerable<string> filteredNames =
      names.Where (n => n.Length >= 4);
    foreach (string name in filteredNames)
      Console.Write (name + "|");
  }
}

// RESULT: Dick|Harry|
```

NOTE

If you are unfamiliar with C#'s lambda expressions, extension methods, or implicit typing, visit *www.albahari. com/cs3primer*.

We can further shorten our query by implicitly typing filteredNames:

```
var filteredNames = names.Where (n => n.Length >= 4);
```

Most query operators accept a lambda expression as an argument. The lambda expression helps guide and shape the query. In our example, the lambda expression is as follows:

```
n => n.Length >= 4
```

The input argument corresponds to an input element. In this case, the input argument n represents each name in the array and is of type string. The Where operator requires that the lambda expression return a bool value, which if true, indicates that the element should be included in the output sequence.

In this book, we describe such queries as *lambda queries*. C#
also defines a special syntax for writing queries, called *query
comprehension syntax*. Here's the preceding query expressed
in comprehension syntax:

```
IEnumerable<string> filteredNames =
  from n in names
  where n.Contains ("a")
  select n;
```

Lambda syntax and comprehension syntax are complemen-
tary. In the following sections, we explore each in more
detail.

Lambda Queries

Lambda queries are the most flexible and fundamental. In
this section, we describe how to chain operators to form
more complex queries and introduce several new query
operators.

Chaining Query Operators

To build more complex queries, you add additional query
operators, creating a chain. For example, the following query
extracts all strings containing the letter *a*, sorts them by
length, and then converts the results to uppercase:

```
string[] names = { "Tom","Dick","Harry","Mary","Jay" };

IEnumerable<string> query = names
  .Where   (n => n.Contains ("a"))
  .OrderBy (n => n.Length)
  .Select  (n => n.ToUpper());

foreach (string name in query)
  Console.Write (name + "|");

// RESULT: JAY|MARY|HARRY|
```

Where, OrderBy, and Select are all standard query operators
that resolve to extension methods in the Enumerable class.

We already introduced the `Where` operator, which emits a filtered version of the input sequence. The `OrderBy` operator emits a sorted version of its input sequence; the `Select` method emits a sequence where each input element is transformed or *projected* with a given lambda expression (`n.ToUpper( )`, in this case). Data flows from left to right through the chain of operators, so the data is first filtered, then sorted, then projected.

NOTE

A query operator never alters the input sequence; instead, it returns a new sequence. This is consistent with the *functional programming* paradigm, from which LINQ was inspired.

Here are the signatures of each of these extension methods (with the `OrderBy` signature simplified slightly):

```
static IEnumerable<TSource> Where<TSource> (
  this IEnumerable<TSource> source,
  Func<TSource,bool> predicate)

static IEnumerable<TSource> OrderBy<TSource,TKey> (
  this IEnumerable<TSource> source,
  Func<TSource,TKey> keySelector)

static IEnumerable<TResult> Select<TSource,TResult> (
  this IEnumerable<TSource> source,
  Func<TSource,TResult> selector)
```

When query operators are chained as in this example, the output sequence of one operator is the input sequence of the next. The end result resembles a production line of conveyor belts, as illustrated in Figure 1.

We can construct the identical query *progressively* as follows:

```
var filtered = names.Where    (n => n.Contains ("a"));
var sorted = filtered.OrderBy (n => n.Length);
var finalQuery = sorted.Select (n => n.ToUpper( ));
```

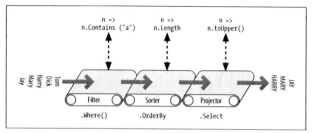

Figure 1. Chaining query operators

`finalQuery` is compositionally identical to the query we had constructed previously. Further, each intermediate step also comprises a valid query that we can execute:

```
foreach (string name in filtered)
  Console.Write (name + "|");        // Harry|Mary|Jay|

Console.WriteLine();
foreach (string name in sorted)
  Console.Write (name + "|");        // Jay|Mary|Harry|

Console.WriteLine();
foreach (string name in finalQuery)
  Console.Write (name + "|");        // JAY|MARY|HARRY|
```

Composing Lambda Expressions

In previous examples, we fed the following lambda expression to the `Where` operator:

```
n => n.Contains ("a")    // Input Type  = string
                         // Return Type = bool
```

NOTE

An expression returning a bool value is called a *predicate*.

The purpose of the lambda expression depends on the particular query operator. With the `Where` operator, it indicates whether an element should be included in the output sequence. In the case of the OrderBy operator, the lambda expression maps each element in the input sequence to its sorting key. With the Select operator, the lambda expression determines how each element in the input sequence is transformed before being fed to the output sequence.

NOTE

A lambda expression in a query operator always works on individual elements in the input sequence—not the sequence as a whole.

The lambda expression you supply acts as a *callback*. The query operator evaluates your lambda expression upon demand—typically once per element in the input sequence. Lambda expressions allow you to feed your own logic into the query operators. This makes the query operators versatile—as well as simple under the hood. Here's the complete implementation of Enumerable.Where, exception handling aside:

```
public static IEnumerable<TSource> Where<TSource> (
  this IEnumerable<TSource> source,
  Func<TSource,bool> predicate)
{
  foreach (TSource element in source)
    if (predicate (element))
      yield return element;
}
```

Lambda expressions and Func signatures

The standard query operators utilize generic Func delegates. Func is a family of general-purpose generic delegates in System.Linq, defined with the following intent:

The type arguments in Func appear in the same order they do in lambda expressions.

Hence, Func<TSource,bool> matches a TSource=>bool lambda expression—one that accepts a TSource argument and returns a bool value.

Similarly, Func<TSource,TResult> matches a TSource=> TResult lambda expression.

Here are all the Func delegate definitions (notice that the return type is always the last generic argument):

```
delegate TResult Func <T> ();

delegate TResult Func <T, TResult>
                 (T arg1);

delegate TResult Func <T1, T2, TResult>
                 (T1 arg1, T2 arg2);

delegate TResult Func <T1, T2, T3, TResult>
                 (T1 arg1, T2 arg2, T3 arg3);

delegate TResult Func <T1, T2, T3, T4, TResult>
                 (T1 arg1, T2 arg2, T3 arg3, T4 arg4);
```

Lambda expressions and element typing

The standard query operators use the following generic type names.

Generic type letter	Meaning
TSource	Element type for the input sequence
TResult	Element type for the output sequence—if different from TSource
TKey	Element type for the *key* used in sorting, grouping, or joining

TSource is determined by the input sequence. TResult and TKey are *inferred from your lambda expression.* For example, consider the signature of the Select query operator:

```
static IEnumerable<TResult> Select<TSource,TResult> (
  this IEnumerable<TSource> source,
  Func<TSource,TResult> selector)
```

Func<TSource,TResult> matches a TSource=>TResult lambda expression—one that maps an *input element* to an *output element*. TSource and TResult are different types, so the lambda expression can change the type of each element. Further, the lambda expression *determines the output sequence type*. The following query uses Select to transform string type elements to integer type elements:

```
string[] names = { "Tom","Dick","Harry","Mary","Jay" };
IEnumerable<int> query = names.Select (n => n.Length);

foreach (int length in query)
  Console.Write (length);        // 34543
```

The compiler *infers* the type of TResult from the return value of the lambda expression. In this case, TResult is inferred to be of type int.

Natural Ordering

The original ordering of elements within an input sequence is significant in LINQ. Some query operators, such as Take, Skip, and Reverse, rely on this behavior. The Take operator outputs the first x elements, discarding the rest; the Skip operator ignores the first x elements, and outputs the rest; the Reverse operator reverses the order of elements in the sequence.

Operators such as Where and Select preserve the original ordering of the input sequence. LINQ preserves the ordering of elements in the input sequence wherever possible.

Other Operators

Not all query operators return a sequence. The *element* operators extract one element from the input sequence; examples are First, Last, Single, and ElementAt:

```
int[] numbers    = { 10, 9, 8, 7, 6 };
int firstNumber  = numbers.First( );          // 10
int lastNumber   = numbers.Last( );           // 6
int secondNumber = numbers.ElementAt (1);     // 9
```

The *aggregation* operators return a scalar value, usually of numeric type:

```
int count = numbers.Count();    // 5;
int min = numbers.Min();        // 6;
```

The *quantifiers* return a bool value:

```
bool hasTheNumberNine = numbers.Contains (9);    // true
bool hasMoreThanZeroElements = numbers.Any();    // true
bool hasAnOddElement = numbers.Any
                        (n => n % 2 == 1);        // true
```

Because these operators don't return a collection, you can't call further operators on their results. In other words, they must appear as the last operator in a query (or subquery).

Some query operators accept two input sequences. Examples are Concat, which appends one sequence to another, and Union, which does the same but with duplicates removed. The joining operators also fall into this category.

Comprehension Queries

C# provides a syntactic shortcut for writing LINQ queries, called *query comprehension syntax*, or simply *query syntax*.

In the preceding section, we wrote a query to extract strings containing the letter *a*, sorted by length, and converted to uppercase. Here's the same query in comprehension syntax:

```
string[] names = { "Tom","Dick","Harry","Mary","Jay" };

IEnumerable<string> query =
  from    n in names
  where   n.Contains ("a")    // Filter elements
  orderby n.Length            // Sort elements
  select  n.ToUpper();        // Project each element

  foreach (string name in query)
    Console.Write (name + "/");

// RESULT: JAY/MARY/HARRY/
```

A comprehension query always starts with a from clause and ends with either a select or group clause. The from clause declares an *iteration variable* (in this case, n), which you can think of as traversing the input collection—rather like foreach. Figure 2 illustrates the complete syntax.

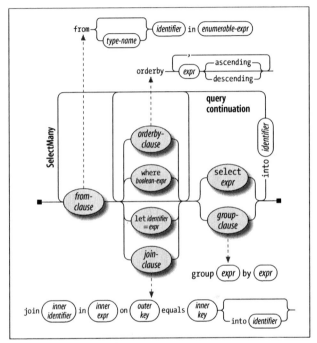

Figure 2. Query comprehension syntax

The compiler processes comprehension queries by translating them to lambda syntax. It does this in a fairly mechanical fashion—much like it translates foreach statements into calls to GetEnumerator and MoveNext. This means that anything you can write in comprehension syntax you can also write in lambda syntax. The compiler translates our example query into the following:

```
IEnumerable<string> query = names
  .Where   (n => n.Contains ("a"))
  .OrderBy (n => n.Length)
  .Select  (n => n.ToUpper( ));
```

The Where, OrderBy, and Select operators then resolve using
the same rules that would apply if the query were written in
lambda syntax. In this case, they bind to extension methods
in the Enumerable class because the System.Linq namespace is
imported and names implements IEnumerable<string>. The
compiler doesn't specifically favor the Enumerable class, however, when translating comprehension queries. You can think
of the compiler as mechanically injecting the words "Where,"
"OrderBy," and "Select" into the statement, and then compiling it as though you'd typed the method names yourself. This
offers flexibility in how they resolve. The operators in the
LINQ to SQL queries that we'll write in later sections, for
instance, will bind instead to extension methods in Queryable.

WARNING

Without the using System.Linq directive, this query will
not compile because the Where, OrderBy, and Select methods will have nowhere to bind. Comprehension queries
cannot compile unless you import a namespace (or write
an instance method for every query operator!).

Iteration Variables

The identifier immediately following the from keyword syntax is called the *iteration variable*. In our examples, the iteration variable n appears in every clause in the query. And yet,
the variable actually enumerates over a *different* sequence
with each clause:

```
from    n in names          // n is our iteration variable
where   n.Contains ("a")    // n = directly from the array
orderby n.Length            // n = after being filtered
select  n.ToUpper( )        // n = after being sorted
```

This becomes clear when we examine the compiler's mechanical translation to lambda syntax:

```
names.Where   (n => n.Contains ("a"))
     .OrderBy (n => n.Length)
     .Select  (n => n.ToUpper())
```

Each instance of n is privately scoped to each lambda expression.

Query Syntax Versus SQL Syntax

LINQ comprehension syntax looks superficially like SQL syntax, yet the two are very different. A LINQ query boils down to a C# expression, and so it follows standard C# rules. For example, with LINQ you cannot use a variable before you declare it. In SQL, you reference a table alias in the SELECT clause before defining it in a FROM clause.

A subquery in LINQ is just another C# expression and so requires no special syntax. Subqueries in SQL are subject to special rules.

With LINQ, data logically flows from left to right through the query. With SQL, the order is more random.

A LINQ query comprises a conveyor belt, or *pipeline*, of operators that accept and emit *ordered sequences*. An SQL query comprises a *network* of clauses that work mostly with *unordered sets*.

Query Syntax Versus Lambda Syntax

Comprehension and lambda syntax each have advantages.

Comprehension syntax is much simpler for queries that involve any of the following:

- A let clause for introducing a new variable alongside the iteration variable
- SelectMany, Join, or GroupJoin followed by an outer iteration variable reference

(We describe the `let` clause in the upcoming "Composition Strategies" section and `SelectMany`, `Join`, and `GroupJoin` in the upcoming "Projecting" and "Joining" sections.)

The middle ground is queries that involve the simple use of `Where`, `OrderBy`, and `Select`. Either syntax works well; the choice here is largely personal.

For queries that comprise a single operator, lambda syntax is shorter and less cluttered.

Finally, there are many operators that have no query comprehension keyword. These require that you use lambda syntax—at least in part, meaning any operator outside of the following:

```
Where, Select, SelectMany
OrderBy, ThenBy, OrderByDescending, ThenByDescending
Group, Join, GroupJoin
```

Mixed Syntax Queries

If a query operator has no comprehension support, you can mix comprehension and lambda syntax. The only restriction is that each comprehension component must be complete (i.e., start with a `from` clause and end with a `select` or `group` clause).

For example:

```
int count = (from name in names
             where n.Contains ("a")
             select name
            ).Count();
```

There are times when mixed syntax queries offer the highest "bang for the buck" by far in terms of function and simplicity. It's important not to unilaterally favor either comprehension or lambda syntax; otherwise, you'll be unable to write mixed syntax queries without feeling a sense of failure!

Deferred Execution

An important feature of most query operators is that they execute not when constructed, but when *enumerated* (in other words, when `MoveNext` is called on its enumerator). Consider the following query:

```
var numbers = new List<int>( );
numbers.Add (1);

// Build query
IEnumerable<int> query = numbers.Select (n => n * 10);
numbers.Add (2);     // Sneak in an extra element

foreach (int n in query)
  Console.Write (n + "|");          // 10|20|
```

The extra number that we sneaked into the list *after* constructing the query is included in the result because it's not until the `foreach` statement runs that any filtering or sorting takes place. This is called *deferred* or *lazy* evaluation. All standard query operators provide deferred execution, with the following exceptions:

- Operators that return a single element or scalar value, such as `First` or `Count`
- The following *conversion operators*:

    `ToArray`, `ToList`, `ToDictionary`, `ToLookup`

These operators cause immediate query execution because their result types have no mechanism for providing deferred execution. The `Count` method, for instance, returns a simple integer, which doesn't then get enumerated. The following query is executed immediately:

```
int matches = numbers.Where (n => n < 2).Count( );  // 1
```

Deferred execution is important because it decouples query *construction* from query *execution*. This allows you to construct a query in several steps, and it makes LINQ to SQL queries possible.

NOTE

Subqueries provide another level of indirection. Everything in a subquery is subject to deferred execution—including aggregation and conversion methods (see the upcoming "Subqueries" section.)

Reevaluation

Deferred execution has another consequence: a deferred execution query is reevaluated when you reenumerate:

```
var numbers = new List<int>() { 1, 2 };

IEnumerable<int> query = numbers.Select (n => n * 10);
foreach (int n in query)
  Console.Write (n + "|");    // 10|20|

numbers.Clear();
foreach (int n in query)
  Console.Write (n + "|");    // <nothing>
```

There are a couple of reasons why reevaluation is sometimes disadvantageous:

- Sometimes you want to "freeze" or cache the results at a certain point in time.

- Some queries are computationally intensive (or rely on querying a remote database), so you don't want to unnecessarily repeat them.

You can defeat reevaluation by calling a conversion operator, such as ToArray or ToList. ToArray copies the output of a query to an array; ToList copies to a generic List<>:

```
var numbers = new List<int>() { 1, 2 };

List<int> timesTen = numbers
  .Select (n => n * 10)
  .ToList();    // Executes immediately into a List<int>

numbers.Clear();
Console.WriteLine (timesTen.Count);    // Still 2
```

Outer Variables

If your query's lambda expressions reference local variables, these variables are *captured* and thus are subject to *outer variable* semantics. This means that what matters is the variable's value at the time the query is executed—not at the time the variable is captured:

```
int[] numbers = { 1, 2 };

int factor = 10;    // We capture this variable below:
var query = numbers.Select (n => n * factor);

factor = 20;        // Change captured variable's value
foreach (int n in query)
  Console.Write (n + "|");    // 20|40|
```

This can be a trap when building up a query within a foreach loop. The following code, for instance, requires the use of a temporary variable to successfully strip all vowels from a string:

```
IEnumerable<char> query = "Not what you might expect";
foreach (char vowel in "aeiou")
{
  char temp = vowel;
  query = query.Where (c => c != temp);
}
```

Without the temporary variable, the query will use the most recent value of vowel ("u") on each successive filter, so only the "u" characters will be removed.

How Deferred Execution Works

Query operators provide deferred execution by returning *decorator* sequences.

Unlike a traditional collection class, such as an array or linked list, a decorator sequence has no backing structure of its own to store elements. Instead, it wraps another sequence that you supply at runtime, to which it maintains a permanent dependency. Whenever you request data from a decorator, it in turn must request data from the wrapped input sequence.

Calling `Where` merely constructs the decorator wrapper sequence, holding a reference to the input sequence, the lambda expression, and any other arguments supplied. The input sequence is enumerated only when the decorator is enumerated.

Figure 3 illustrates the composition of the following query:

```
IEnumerable<int> lessThanTen =
  new int[] { 5, 12, 3 }.Where (n => n < 10);
```

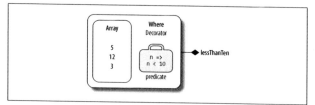

Figure 3. Decorator sequence

When you enumerate `lessThanTen`, you're, in effect, querying the array through the `Where` decorator.

The good news—if you ever want to write your own query operator—is that implementing a decorator sequence is easy with a C# iterator. Here's how you can write your own Select method:

```
static IEnumerable<TResult> Select<TSource,TResult> (
  this IEnumerable<TSource> source,
  Func<TSource,TResult> selector)
{
  foreach (TSource element in source)
    yield return selector (element);
}
```

This method is an iterator by virtue of the yield return statement. Functionally, it's a shortcut for the following:

```
static IEnumerable<TResult> Select<TSource,TResult> (
  this IEnumerable<TSource> source,
  Func<TSource,TResult> selector)
{
  return new SelectSequence (source, selector);
}
```

where *SelectSequence* is a (compiler-written) class whose enumerator encapsulates the logic in the iterator method.

Hence, when you call an operator such as Select or Where, you're doing nothing more than instantiating an enumerable class that decorates the input sequence.

Chaining Decorators

Chaining query operators creates a layering of decorators. Consider the following query:

```
IEnumerable<int> query = new int[] { 5, 12, 3 }
  .Where    (n => n < 10)
  .OrderBy  (n => n)
  .Select   (n => n * 10);
```

Each query operator instantiates a new decorator that wraps the previous sequence—rather like a Russian doll. The object model of this query is illustrated in Figure 4. Note that this object model is fully constructed prior to any enumeration.

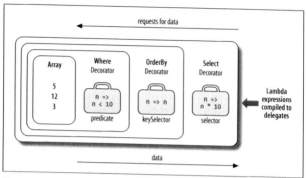

Figure 4. Layered decorator sequences

When you enumerate query, you're querying the original array, transformed through a layering or chain of decorators.

NOTE

Adding ToList onto the end of this query would cause the preceding operators to execute right away, collapsing the whole object model into a single list.

A feature of deferred execution is that you build the identical object model if you compose the query progressively:

```
IEnumerable<int>
  source   = new int[] { 5, 12, 3 },
  filtered = source   .Where   (n => n < 10),
  sorted   = filtered .OrderBy (n => n),
  query    = sorted   .Select  (n => n * 10);
```

How Queries Are Executed

Here are the results of enumerating the preceding query:

```
foreach (int n in query)
  Console.Write (n + "/");     // 30/50/
```

Behind the scenes, the foreach calls GetEnumerator on Select's decorator (the last or outermost operator), which kicks everything off. The result is a chain of enumerators that structurally mirrors the chain of decorator sequences. Figure 5 illustrates the flow of execution as enumeration proceeds.

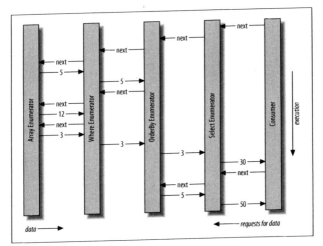

Figure 5. Execution of a local query

Recall that a query is like a production line of conveyor belts. Extending this analogy, we can say a LINQ query is a lazy production line, where the conveyor belts and lambda workers roll elements only upon *demand*. Constructing a query creates a production line—with everything in place—but with nothing rolling. Then when the consumer requests an element (enumerates over the query), the rightmost conveyor belt activates; this in turn triggers the others to roll—as and when input sequence elements are needed. LINQ follows a demand-driven *pull* model, rather than a supply-driven *push* model. This is important—as we'll see later—in allowing LINQ to scale to querying SQL databases.

Subqueries

A *subquery* is a query contained within another query's lambda expression. The following example uses a subquery to sort musicians by their last name:

```
string[] musos =
  { "David Gilmour", "Roger Waters", "Rick Wright" };

IEnumerable<string> query =
  musos.OrderBy (m => m.Split().Last());
```

`m.Split` converts each string into a collection of words, upon which we then call the `Last` query operator. `Last` is the subquery; query references the *outer query*.

Subqueries are permitted because you can put any valid C# expression on the right side of a lambda. A subquery is simply another C# expression, meaning that the rules for subqueries are a consequence of the rules for lambda expressions (and the behavior of query operators in general).

A subquery is privately scoped to the enclosing expression and is able to reference the outer lambda argument (or iteration variable in comprehension syntax).

`Last` is a very simple subquery. The next query retrieves all strings in an array whose length matches that of the shortest string:

```
string[] names = { "Tom","Dick","Harry","Mary","Jay" };

IEnumerable<string> outerQuery = names
  .Where (n => n.Length ==
    names.OrderBy (n2 => n2.Length)
         .Select  (n2 => n2.Length).First()
  );

// RESULT: Tom, Jay
```

Here's the same thing in comprehension syntax:

```
IEnumerable<string> comprehension =
  from   n in names
  where  n.Length ==
    (from n2 in names
     orderby n2.Length
     select n2.Length).First()
  select n;
```

Because the outer iteration variable (n) is in scope for a subquery, we cannot reuse n as the subquery's iteration variable.

A subquery is executed whenever the enclosing lambda expression is evaluated. This means a subquery is executed upon demand, at the discretion of the outer query. You could say that execution proceeds from the *outside in*. Local queries follow this model literally; interpreted queries (e.g., LINQ to SQL queries) follow this model *conceptually*.

The subquery executes as and when required to feed the outer query. In our example, the subquery (the top conveyor belt in Figure 6) executes once for every outer loop iteration.

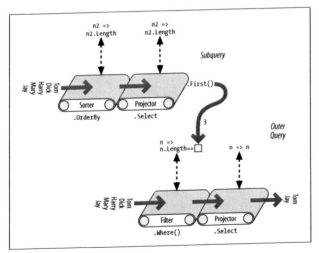

Figure 6. Subquery composition

The preceding subquery can be expressed more succinctly as follows:

```
IEnumerable<string> query =
  from  n in names
  where n.Length ==
        names.OrderBy (n2 => n2.Length).First( ).Length
  select n;
```

With the Min aggregation function, it can be simplified further:

```
IEnumerable<string> query =
  from  n in names
  where n.Length == names.Min (n2 => n2.Length)
  select n;
```

In the upcoming "Interpreted Queries" section, we describe how remote sources such as SQL tables can be queried. Our example makes an ideal LINQ to SQL query because it would be processed as a unit, requiring only one round trip to the database server. This query, however, is inefficient for a local collection because the subquery is recalculated on each outer loop iteration. We can avoid this inefficiency by running the subquery separately (so that it's no longer a subquery):

```
int shortest = names.Min (n => n.Length);

IEnumerable<string> query = from  n in names
                            where n.Length == shortest
                            select n;
```

NOTE

Factoring out subqueries in this manner is nearly always desirable when querying local collections. An exception is when the subquery is *correlated*, meaning that it references the outer iteration variable. We explore correlated subqueries later in the "Projecting" section.

Subqueries and Deferred Execution

An element or aggregation operator such as `First` or `Count` in a subquery doesn't force the *outer* query into immediate execution—deferred execution still holds for the outer query. This is because subqueries are called *indirectly*—through a delegate in the case of a local query, or through an expression tree in the case of an interpreted query.

An interesting case arises when you include a subquery within a `Select` expression. In the case of a local query, you're actually *projecting a sequence of queries*—each itself subject to deferred execution. The effect is generally transparent, and it serves to further improve efficiency.

Composition Strategies

In this section, we describe three strategies for building more complex queries:

- Progressive query construction
- Using the `into` keyword
- Wrapping queries

All are *chaining* strategies and produce identical runtime queries.

Progressive Query Building

At the start of the chapter, we demonstrated how you could build a lambda query progressively:

```
var filtered = names.Where (n => n.Contains ("a"));
var sorted = filtered.OrderBy (n => n);
var query = sorted.Select (n => n.ToUpper( ));
```

Because each of the participating query operators returns a decorator sequence, the resultant query is the same chain or layering of decorators that you would get from a single-expression query. There are a couple of potential benefits, however, to building queries progressively:

- It can make queries easier to write.
- You can add query operators *conditionally*.

A progressive approach is often useful in comprehension queries. To illustrate, imagine we wanted to use Regex to remove all vowels from a list of names, and then present in alphabetical order those whose length is still more than two characters. In lambda syntax, we could write this query as a single expression—by projecting *before* we filter:

```
IEnumerable<string> query = names
  .Select  (n => Regex.Replace (n, "[aeiou]", ""))
  .Where   (n => n.Length > 2)
  .OrderBy (n => n);

RESULT: { "Dck", "Hrry", "Mry" }
```

Translating this directly to comprehension syntax is troublesome because comprehension clauses must appear in where-orderby-select order to be recognized by the compiler. And if we rearranged the query to project last, the result would be different:

```
IEnumerable<string> query =
  from    n in names
  where   n.Length > 2
  orderby n
  select  Regex.Replace (n, "[aeiou]", "");

RESULT: { "Dck", "Hrry", "Jy", "Mry", "Tm" }
```

Fortunately, there are a number of ways to get the original result in comprehension syntax. The first is by querying progressively:

```
IEnumerable<string> query =
  from    n in names
  select  Regex.Replace (n, "[aeiou]", "");

query = from n in query
        where n.Length > 2
        orderby n
        select n;

RESULT: { "Dck", "Hrry", "Mry" }
```

The into Keyword

The into keyword lets you "continue" a query after a projection, and is a shortcut for progressively querying. With into, we can rewrite the preceding query as:

```
IEnumerable<string> query =
   from   n in names
   select Regex.Replace (n, "[aeiou]", "")
   into noVowel
   where noVowel.Length > 2
   orderby noVowel
   select noVowel;
```

NOTE

The into keyword is interpreted in two very different ways in comprehension syntax, depending on context. The meaning we're describing now is for signaling *query continuation* (the other is for signaling a GroupJoin).

The only place you can use into is after a select or group clause. into "restarts" a query, allowing you to introduce fresh where, orderby, and select clauses.

NOTE

Although it's easiest to think of into as restarting a query from the perspective of comprehension syntax, it's *all one query* when translated to its final lambda form. Hence, there's no intrinsic performance hit with into. Nor do you lose any points for its use!

The equivalent of into in lambda syntax is simply a longer chain of operators.

Scoping rules

All query variables are out of scope following an into keyword. The following will not compile:

```
var query =
  from n1 in names
  select n1.ToUpper()
  into n2
  where n1.Contains ("x")   // Illegal: n1 out of scope.
  select n2;
```

To see why, consider how this maps to lambda syntax:

```
var query = names
  .Select (n1 => n1.ToUpper())
  .Where  (n2 => n1.Contains ("x"));
```

The original name (n1) is lost by the time the Where filter runs. Where's input sequence contains only uppercase names, so it cannot filter based on n1.

Wrapping Queries

A query built progressively can be formulated into a single statement by wrapping one query around another. In general terms:

```
var tempQuery = tempQueryExpr
var finalQuery = from ... in tempQuery ...
```

can be reformulated as:

```
var finalQuery = from ... in (tempQueryExpr)
```

Wrapping is semantically identical to progressive query building or using the into keyword (without the intermediate variable). The end result in all cases is a linear chain of query operators. For example, consider the following query:

```
IEnumerable<string> query =
  from  n in names
  select Regex.Replace (n, "[aeiou]", "");
```

```
query = from n in query
        where n.Length > 2
        orderby n
        select n;
```

Reformulated in wrapped form, it's this:

```
IEnumerable<string> query =
  from n1 in
  (
    from  n2 in names
    select Regex.Replace (n2, "[aeiou]", "")
  )
  where n1.Length > 2 orderby n1 select n1;
```

When converted to lambda syntax, the result is the same linear chain of operators as in previous examples:

```
IEnumerable<string> query = names
  .Select  (n => Regex.Replace (n, "[aeiou]", ""))
  .Where   (n => n.Length > 2)
  .OrderBy (n => n);
```

(The compiler does not emit the final .Select (n => n) because it's redundant.)

Wrapped queries can be confusing because they resemble the subqueries we wrote earlier: both have the concept of an inner and outer query. When converted to lambda syntax, however, you can see that wrapping is simply a strategy for sequentially chaining operators. The end result bears no resemblance to a subquery, which embeds an inner query within the *lambda expression* of another.

Returning to a previous analogy, when wrapping, the "inner" query amounts to the *preceding conveyor belts*. In contrast, a subquery rides above a conveyor belt and is activated upon demand through the conveyor belt's lambda worker (as illustrated earlier in Figure 6).

Projection Strategies

Object Initializers

So far, all our select clauses have projected scalar element types. With C# *object initializers*, you can project into more complex types. For example, suppose, as a first step in a query, we want to strip vowels from a list of names while still retaining the original versions alongside for the benefit of subsequent queries. We can write the following class to assist:

```
class TempProjectionItem
{
  public string Original;   // Original name
  public string Vowelless;  // Vowel-stripped name
}
```

and then project into it with object initializers:

```
string[] names = { "Tom","Dick","Harry","Mary","Jay" };

IEnumerable<TempProjectionItem> temp =
  from n in names
  select new TempProjectionItem
  {
    Original  = n,
    Vowelless = Regex.Replace (n, "[aeiou]", "")
  };
```

The result is of type IEnumerable<TempProjectionItem>, which we can subsequently query:

```
IEnumerable<string> query =
  from   item in temp
  where  item.Vowelless.Length > 2
  select item.Original;

// RESULT: Dick, Harry, Mary
```

Anonymous Types

Anonymous types allow you to structure your intermediate results without writing special classes. We can eliminate the

`TempProjectionItem` class in our previous example with anonymous types:

```
var intermediate = from n in names
  select new
  {
    Original = n,
    Vowelless = Regex.Replace (n, "[aeiou]", "")
  };

IEnumerable<string> query =
  from    item in intermediate
  where   item.Vowelless.Length > 2
  select item.Original;
```

This gives the same result as the previous example, but without needing to write a one-off class. The compiler does the job instead, writing a temporary class with fields that match the structure of our projection. This means, however, that the `intermediate` query has the following type:

```
IEnumerable <random-compiler-produced-name>
```

The only way we can declare a variable of this type is with the `var` keyword. In this case, `var` is more than just a clutter reduction device; it's a necessity.

We can write the whole query more succinctly with the `into` keyword:

```
var query = from n in names
  select new
  {
    Original = n,
    Vowelless = Regex.Replace (n, "[aeiou]", "")
  }
  into temp
  where temp.Vowelless.Length > 2
  select temp.Original;
```

Query comprehension syntax provides a shortcut for writing this kind of query: the `let` keyword.

The let Keyword

The `let` keyword introduces a new variable alongside the iteration variable.

With `let`, we can write a query extracting strings whose length excluding vowels exceeds two characters as follows:

```
string[] names = { "Tom","Dick","Harry","Mary","Jay" };

IEnumerable<string> query =
  from n in names
  let vowelless = Regex.Replace (n, "[aeiou]", "")
  where vowelless.Length > 2
  orderby vowelless
  select n;        // Thanks to let, n is still in scope.
```

The compiler resolves a `let` clause by projecting into a temporary anonymous type that contains both the iteration variable and the new expression variable. In other words, the compiler translates this query into the preceding example.

`let` accomplishes two things:

- It projects new elements alongside existing elements.
- It allows an expression to be used repeatedly in a query without being rewritten.

The `let` approach is particularly advantageous in this example because it allows the `select` clause to project either the original name (n) or its vowel-removed version (v).

You can have any number of `let` statements before or after a `where` statement (see Figure 2, earlier). A `let` statement can reference variables introduced in earlier `let` statements (subject to the boundaries imposed by an `into` clause). `let` *reprojects* all existing variables transparently.

A `let` expression need not evaluate a scalar type: sometimes it's useful to have it evaluate to a subsequence, for instance.

Interpreted Queries

LINQ provides two parallel architectures: *local* queries for local object collections, and *interpreted* queries for remote data sources. So far, we've examined the architecture of local queries, which operate over collections implementing IEnumerable<>. Local queries resolve to query operators in the Enumerable class, which in turn resolve to chains of decorator sequences. The delegates that they accept—whether expressed in comprehension syntax, lambda syntax, or traditional delegates—are fully local to Intermediate Language (IL) code just as any other C# method.

By contrast, interpreted queries are *descriptive*. They operate over sequences that implement IQueryable<>, and they resolve to the query operators in the Queryable class, which emit *expression trees* that are interpreted at runtime.

NOTE

The query operators in Enumerable can actually work with IQueryable<> sequences. The difficulty is that the resultant queries always execute locally on the client—this is why a second set of query operators is provided in the Queryable class.

There are two IQueryable implementations in the .NET Framework:

- LINQ to SQL
- LINQ to Entities

In addition, the AsQueryable extension method generates an IQueryable wrapper around an ordinary enumerable collection. We describe AsQueryable in the upcoming "Building Query Expressions" section.

In this section, we'll use LINQ to SQL to illustrate interpreted query architecture.

<hr/>

NOTE

IQueryable<> is an extension of IEnumerable<> with additional methods for constructing expression trees. Most of the time, you can ignore the details of these methods; they're called indirectly by the Framework. The upcoming "Building Query Expressions" section covers IQueryable<> in more detail.

<hr/>

Suppose we create a simple customer table in SQL Server and populate it with a few names using the following SQL script:

```sql
create table Customer
(
  ID int not null primary key,
  Name varchar(30)
)
insert Customer values (1, 'Tom')
insert Customer values (2, 'Dick')
insert Customer values (3, 'Harry')
insert Customer values (4, 'Mary')
insert Customer values (5, 'Jay')
```

With this table in place, we can write an interpreted LINQ query in C# to retrieve customers whose names contain the letter *a*, as follows:

```csharp
using System;
using System.Linq;
using System.Data.Linq;
using System.Data.Linq.Mapping;

[Table] public class Customer
{
  [Column(IsPrimaryKey=true)] public int ID;
  [Column]                    public string Name;
}

class Test
{
```

```
static void Main()
{
  var dataContext = new DataContext ("cx string...");

  Table<Customer> customers =
    dataContext.GetTable <Customer>();

  IQueryable<string> query = from c in customers
    where   c.Name.Contains ("a")
    orderby c.Name.Length
    select  c.Name.ToUpper();

  foreach (string name in query)
    Console.WriteLine (name);
}
}
```

LINQ to SQL translates this query into the following SQL:

```
SELECT UPPER([t0].[Name]) AS [value]
FROM [Customer] AS [t0]
WHERE [t0].[Name] LIKE '%a%'
ORDER BY LEN([t0].[Name])
```

with the following end result:

```
JAY
MARY
HARRY
```

How Interpreted Queries Work

Let's examine how the preceding query is processed.

First, the compiler converts the query from comprehension to lambda syntax. This is done exactly as it is with local queries:

```
IQueryable<string> query = customers
  .Where   (n => n.Name.Contains ("a"))
  .OrderBy (n => n.Name.Length)
  .Select  (n => n.Name.ToUpper());
```

Next, the compiler resolves the query operator methods. Here's where local and interpreted queries differ—interpreted queries resolve to query operators in the Queryable class instead of the Enumerable class.

To see why, we need to look at the customers variable, the source upon which the whole query builds. customers is of type Table<>, which implements IQueryable<> (a subtype of IEnumerable<>). This means the compiler has a choice in resolving Where: it could call the extension method in Enumerable, or the following extension method in Queryable:

```
public static IQueryable<TSource> Where<TSource> (
  this IQueryable<TSource> source,
  Expression <Func<TSource,bool>> predicate)
```

The compiler chooses Queryable.Where because its signature is a *more specific match*.

Note that Queryable.Where accepts a predicate wrapped in an Expression<TDelegate> type. This instructs the compiler to translate the supplied lambda expression—in other words, n=>n.Name.Contains("a")—to an *expression tree* rather than a compiled delegate. An expression tree is an object model based on the types in System.Linq.Expressions that can be inspected at runtime (so that LINQ to SQL can later translate it to an SQL statement).

Because Queryable.Where also returns IQueryable<>, the same process follows with the OrderBy and Select operators. The end result is illustrated in Figure 7. In the shaded box is an expression tree describing the entire query, which can be traversed at runtime.

Execution

Interpreted queries follow a deferred execution model—just like local queries. This means that the SQL statement is not generated until you start enumerating the query. Further, enumerating the same query twice results in the database being queried twice.

Under the cover, interpreted queries differ from local queries in how they execute. When you enumerate over an interpreted query, the outermost sequence runs a program that traverses the entire expression tree, processing it as a unit. In our example, LINQ to SQL translates the expression tree to a

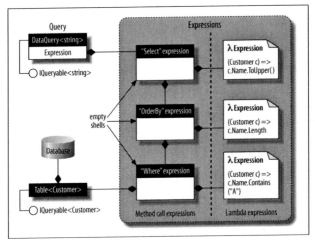

Figure 7. Interpreted query composition

SQL statement, which it then executes, yielding the results as a sequence.

NOTE

To work, LINQ to SQL needs some clues as to the schema of the database. The Table and Column attributes that we applied to the Customer class serve just this function. The upcoming "LINQ to SQL" section describes these attributes in more detail.

We said previously that a LINQ query is like a production line. When you enumerate an IQueryable conveyor belt, though, it doesn't start up the whole production line, as it does with a local query. Instead, just the IQueryable belt starts up, with a special enumerator that calls upon a production manager. The manager reviews the entire production line—which consists not of compiled code, but of dummies (method call expressions) with instructions pasted to their foreheads (lambda expression trees). The manager then traverses all the expressions, in this case transcribing them to a single piece of paper (an SQL statement)—which it then executes—feeding the results back to the consumer. Only one belt turns; the rest of the production line is a network of empty shells, existing just to describe what has to be done.

This has some practical implications. For instance, with local queries, you can write your own query methods (fairly easily with iterators) and then use them to supplement the pre-defined set. With remote queries, this is difficult, even undesirable. If you wrote a `MyWhere` extension method accepting `IQueryable<>`, it would be like putting your own dummy into the production line. The production manager wouldn't know what to do with your dummy. Even if you intervened at this stage, your solution would be hard wired to a particular provider, such as LINQ to SQL, and would not work with other `IQueryable` implementations. Part of the benefit of having a standard set of methods in `Queryable` is that they define a *standard vocabulary* for querying *any* remote collection. As soon as you try to extend the vocabulary, you're no longer interoperable.

Another consequence of this model is that an `IQueryable` provider may be unable to cope with some queries—even if you stick to the standard methods. LINQ to SQL, for instance, is limited by the capabilities of the database server; some LINQ queries have no SQL translation. If you're familiar with SQL, you'll have a good intuition for what these are, although at times, you will have to experiment to see what causes a runtime error; it can be surprising what *does* work! Your chances with LINQ to SQL are best with the latest version of Microsoft SQL Server.

AsEnumerable

`Enumerable.AsEnumerable` is the simplest of all query operators. Here's its complete definition:

```
public static IEnumerable<TSource> AsEnumerable<TSource>
                 (this IEnumerable<TSource> source)
{
    return source;
}
```

Its purpose is to cast an IQueryable<T> sequence to IEnumerable<T>, forcing subsequent query operators to bind to Enumerable operators instead of Queryable operators. This causes the remainder of the query to execute locally.

To illustrate, suppose we had a MedicalArticles table in SQL Server and wanted to use LINQ to SQL to retrieve all articles on influenza whose abstract contained fewer than 100 words. For the latter predicate, we need a regular expression:

```
Regex wordCounter = new Regex (@"\b(\w|[-'])+\b");

var query = dataContext.MedicalArticles
  .Where (article => article.Topic == "influenza" &&
    wordCounter.Matches (article.Abstract).Count < 100);
```

The problem is that SQL Server doesn't support regular expressions, so LINQ to SQL throws an exception, complaining that the query cannot be translated to SQL. We can solve this by querying in two steps: first retrieve all articles on influenza through a LINQ to SQL query, and then filter *locally* for abstracts fewer than 100 words:

```
Regex wordCounter = new Regex (@"\b(\w|[-'])+\b");

IEnumerable<MedicalArticle> sqlQuery =
  dataContext.MedicalArticles
  .Where (article => article.Topic == "influenza");

IEnumerable<MedicalArticle> localQuery = sqlQuery
  .Where (article =>
    wordCounter.Matches (article.Abstract).Count < 100);
```

Because sqlQuery is of type IEnumerable<MedicalArticle>, the second query binds to the local query operators, forcing that part of the filtering to run on the client.

With AsEnumerable, we can do the same in a single query:

```
Regex wordCounter = new Regex (@"\b(\w|[-'])+\b");

var query = dataContext.MedicalArticles
  .Where (article => article.Topic == "influenza")
  .AsEnumerable( )
  .Where (article =>
    wordCounter.Matches (article.Abstract).Count < 100);
```

An alternative to calling AsEnumerable is to call ToArray or ToList. The advantage of AsEnumerable is that it doesn't force immediate query execution, nor does it create any storage structure.

NOTE

Moving query processing from the database server to the client can hurt performance, especially if it means retrieving more rows. A more efficient (though more complex) way to solve our example would be to use SQL CLR integration to expose a function on the database that implemented the regular expression.

LINQ to SQL

Throughout this book, we rely on LINQ to SQL to demonstrate interpreted queries. This section examines the key features of this technology.

LINQ to SQL Entity Classes

LINQ to SQL allows you to use any class to represent data, as long as you decorate it with appropriate attributes. Here's a simple example:

```
[Table]
public class Customer
{
  [Column(IsPrimaryKey=true)]
  public int ID;
```

```
    [Column]
    public string Name;
}
```

The [Table] attribute, in the System.Data.Linq.Mapping
namespace, tells LINQ to SQL that an object of this type represents a row in a database table. By default, it assumes the
table name matches the class name; if this is not the case,
you can specify the table name as follows:

```
[Table (Name="Customers")]
```

A class decorated with the [Table] attribute is called an *entity*
in LINQ to SQL. To be useful, its structure must closely—or
exactly—match that of a database table, making it a low-
level construct.

The [Column] attribute flags a field or property that maps to a
column in a table. If the column name differs from the field or
property name, you can specify the column name as follows:

```
[Column (Name="FullName")]
public string Name;
```

The IsPrimaryKey property in the [Column] attribute indicates that the column partakes in the table's primary key. It
is required for maintaining object identity, as well as for
allowing updates to be written back to the database.

Instead of defining public fields, you can define public properties in conjunction with private fields. This allows you to
write validation logic into the property accessors. If you take
this route, you can optionally instruct LINQ to SQL to
bypass your property accessors and write to the field directly
when populating from the database:

```
string _name;

[Column (Storage="_name")]
public string Name
{ get { return _name; } set { _name = value; } }
```

Column(Storage="_name") tells LINQ to SQL to write directly to the _name field (rather than the Name property) when populating the entity. LINQ to SQL's use of reflection allows the field to be private—as in this example.

DataContext

Once you've defined entity classes, you start querying by instantiating a DataContext object and then calling GetTable on it. The following example uses the Customer class defined originally:

```
var dataContext = new DataContext ("cx string...");
Table<Customer> customers =
  dataContext.GetTable <Customer>();

// Print number of rows in table
Console.WriteLine (customers.Count());

// Retrieves Customer with ID of 2
Customer cust = customers.Single (c => c.ID == 2);
```

NOTE

The Single operator is ideal for retrieving a row by primary key. Unlike First, it throws an exception if more than one element is returned.

A DataContext object does two things. First, it acts as a factory for generating tables that you can query. Second, it keeps track of any changes that you make to your entities so that you can write them back:

```
var dataContext = new DataContext ("cx string...");
Table<Customer> customers =
  dataContext.GetTable <Customer>();
Customer cust = customers.OrderBy (c => c.Name).First();
cust.Name = "Updated Name";
dataContext.SubmitChanges();
```

A `DataContext` object keeps track of all the entities it instantiates, so it can feed the same ones back to you whenever you request the same rows in a table. In other words, in its lifetime a `DataContext` object will never emit two separate entities that refer to the same row in a table (where a row is identified by primary key).

NOTE

Set `ObjectTrackingEnabled` to false on the `DataContext` object to disable this behavior. (Disabling object tracking also prevents you from submitting updates to the data.)

To illustrate object tracking, suppose the customer whose name is alphabetically first also has the lowest ID. In the following example, a and b will reference the same object:

```
var dataContext = new DataContext ("cx string...");
Table<Customer> customers =
  dataContext.GetTable <Customer>( );

Customer a = customers.OrderBy (c => c.Name).First( );
Customer b = customers.OrderBy (c => c.ID).First( );
```

This has a couple of interesting consequences. First, consider what happens when LINQ to SQL encounters the second query. It starts by querying the database and obtaining a single row. It then reads the primary key of this row and performs a lookup in the `DataContext`'s entity cache. Seeing a match, it returns the existing object, *without updating any values*. So, if another user had just updated that customer's `Name` in the database, the new value would be ignored. This is essential for avoiding unexpected side effects (the `Customer` object could be in use elsewhere) and also for managing concurrency. If you had altered properties on the `Customer` object and not yet called `SubmitChanges`, you wouldn't want your properties automatically overwritten.

The second consequence is that you cannot explicitly project into an entity type—to select a subset of the row's columns—without causing trouble. For example, if you wanted to retrieve only a customer's name, any of the following approaches is valid:

```
customers.Select (c => c.Name);
customers.Select (c => new { Name = c.Name } );
customers.Select (c => new
                  MyCustomType { Name = c.Name } );
```

The following, however, is not:

```
customers.Select (c => new Customer { Name = c.Name } );
```

This is because the Customer entities will end up partially populated. So, the next time you perform a query that requests *all* customer columns, you get the same cached Customer objects with only the Name property populated.

Automatic Entity Generation

Because LINQ to SQL entity classes need to follow the structure of their underlying tables, it's likely that you'll want to generate them automatically from an existing database schema. You can do this either via the SqlMetal command-line tool or the LINQ to SQL designer in Visual Studio. These tools generate entities as partial classes so that you can incorporate additional logic in separate files.

As a bonus, you also get a strongly typed DataContext class, which is simply a subclassed DataContext with properties that return tables of each entity type. It saves you calling GetTable:

```
var dataContext = new MyTypedDataContext ("...");
Table<Customer> customers = dataContext.Customers;
Console.WriteLine (customers.Count());
```

or simply:

```
Console.WriteLine (dataContext.Customers.Count());
```

The LINQ to SQL designer automatically pluralizes identifiers where appropriate. In this example, it's dataContext.Customers and not dataContext.Customer—even though the SQL table and entity class are both called Customer.

Associations

The entity generation tools perform another useful job. For each relationship defined in your database, properties are automatically generated on each side that query that relationship. For example, suppose we define a customer and purchase table in a one-to-many relationship:

```
create table Customer
(
  ID int not null primary key,
  Name varchar(30) not null
)
```

```
create table Purchase
(
  ID int not null primary key,
  CustomerID int references Customer (ID),
  Description varchar(30) not null,
  Price decimal not null
)
```

If we use automatically generated entity classes, we can write these queries as follows:

```
var dataContext = new MyTypedDataContext ("...");

// Retrieve all purchases made by the first
// customer (alphabetically):

Customer cust1 = dataContext.Customers
  .OrderBy (c => c.Name).First();

foreach (Purchase p in cust1.Purchases)
  Console.WriteLine (p.Price);

// Retrieve customer who made the lowest value purchase:

Purchase cheapest = dataContext.Purchases
  .OrderBy (p => p.Price).First();

Customer cust2 = cheapest.Customer;
```

Further, if cust1 and cust2 happened to refer to the same customer, c1 and c2 would *refer to the same object*: cust1==cust2 would return true.

Let's examine the signature of the automatically generated Purchases property on the Customer entity:

```
[Association (Storage="_Purchases",
             OtherKey="CustomerID")]
public EntitySet <Purchase> Purchases
{ get {...} set {...} }
```

An EntitySet is like a predefined query with a built-in Where clause that extracts related entities. The [Association] attribute gives LINQ to SQL the information it needs to write the query. As with any other type of query, you get deferred execution. This means that with an EntitySet, the

---

query doesn't execute until you enumerate over the related collection.

Here's the `Purchases.Customer` property on the other side of the relationship:

```
[Association (Storage="_Customer",
              ThisKey="CustomerID",
              IsForeignKey=true)]
public Customer Customer { get {...} set {...} }
```

Although the property is of type `Customer`, its underlying field (`_Customer`) is of type `EntityRef`. The `EntityRef` type implements deferred loading, so the related `Customer` is not retrieved from the database until you actually ask for it.

Deferred Execution with LINQ to SQL

LINQ to SQL queries are subject to deferred execution, just like local queries, allowing you to build queries progressively. There is one aspect, however, in which LINQ to SQL has special deferred execution semantics, and that is when a subquery appears inside a `Select` expression:

- With local queries, you get double deferred execution because from a functional perspective, you're selecting a sequence of *queries*. So, if you enumerate the outer result sequence, but never enumerate the inner sequences, the subquery will never execute.

- With LINQ to SQL, the subquery is executed at the same time as the main outer query. This avoids excessive round-tripping.

For example, the following query executes in a single round trip upon reaching the first `foreach` statement:

```
var dataContext = new MyTypedDataContext ("...");

var query = from c in dataContext.Customers
            select
                from p in c.Purchases
                select new { c.Name, p.Price };
```

```
foreach (var customerPurchaseResults in query)
  foreach (var namePrice in customerPurchaseResults)
    Console.WriteLine (namePrice.Name + " spent " +
                        namePrice.Price);
```

Any EntitySets that you explicitly project are fully populated in a single round trip:

```
var query = from c in dataContext.Customers
            select new { c.Name, c.Purchases };

foreach (var row in query)
  foreach (Purchase p in row.Purchases)
    Console.WriteLine (row.Name + " spent " + p.Price);
```

But if we enumerate EntitySet properties without first having projected, deferred execution rules apply. In the following example, LINQ to SQL executes another Purchases query
on each loop iteration:

```
foreach (Customer c in dataContext.Customers)
  foreach (Purchase p in c.Purchases)     // + Round-trip
    Console.WriteLine (c.Name + " spent " + p.Price);
```

This model is advantageous when you want to *selectively*
execute the inner loop, based on a test that can be per-
formed only on the client:

```
foreach (Customer c in dataContext.Customers)
  if (myWebService.HasBadCreditHistory (c.ID))
    foreach (Purchase p in c.Purchases)  // + Round trip
      Console.WriteLine (...);
```

We explore Select subqueries in more detail in the upcoming "Projecting" section.

DataLoadOptions

The DataLoadOptions class has two distinct uses:

- It lets you specify, in advance, a filter for EntitySet associations (AssociateWith).

- It lets you request that certain EntitySets be eagerly
  loaded to lessen round-tripping (LoadWith).

Specifying a filter in advance

Here's how to use `DataLoadOptions`'s `AssociateWith` method:

```
DataLoadOptions options = new DataLoadOptions();
options.AssociateWith <Customer>
  (c => c.Purchases.Where (p => p.Price > 1000));
dataContext.LoadOptions = options;
```

This instructs the `DataContext` instance to always filter a `Customer`'s `Purchases` using the given predicate.

`AssociateWith` doesn't change deferred execution semantics. It simply instructs to implicitly add a particular filter to the equation when a particular relationship is used.

Eager loading

The second use for a `DataLoadOptions` is to request that certain `EntitySets` be eagerly loaded with their parents. For instance, suppose you wanted to load all customers and their purchases in a single SQL round trip. The following does exactly this:

```
DataLoadOptions options = new DataLoadOptions();
options.LoadWith <Customer> (c => c.Purchases);
dataContext.LoadOptions = options;

foreach (Customer c in dataContext.Customers)
  foreach (Purchase p in c.Purchases)
    Console.WriteLine (c.Name + " bought a " +
                       p.Description);
```

This instructs that whenever a `Customer` is retrieved, its `Purchases` should be too at the same time. You can also request that grandchildren be included:

```
options.LoadWith <Customer> (c => c.Purchases);
options.LoadWith <Purchase> (p => p.PurchaseItems);
```

You can combine `LoadWith` with `AssociateWith`. The following instructs that whenever a customer is retrieved, its *high-value* purchases should be retrieved in the same round trip:

```
options.LoadWith <Customer> (c => c.Purchases);
options.AssociateWith <Customer>
  (c => c.Purchases.Where (p => p.Price > 1000));
```

Updates

LINQ to SQL also keeps track of changes you make to your entities and allows you to write them back to the database by calling SubmitChanges on the DataContext object. The Table<> class provides InsertOnSubmit and DeleteOnSubmit methods for inserting and deleting rows in a table; here's how to add a row to a table:

```
var dataContext = new MyTypedDataContext ("cx string");

Customer cust = new Customer { ID=1000, Name="Bloggs" };
dataContext.Customers.InsertOnSubmit (cust);
dataContext.SubmitChanges();
```

We can later retrieve that row, update it, and then delete it:

```
var dataContext = new MyTypedDataContext ("...");

Customer cust = dataContext.Customers.Single
                   (c => c.ID == 1000);
cust.Name = "Bloggs2";
dataContext.SubmitChanges();       // Updates the customer

dataContext.Customers.DeleteOnSubmit (cust);
dataContext.SubmitChanges();       // Deletes the customer
```

DataContext.SubmitChanges gathers all the changes that were made to its entities since the DataContext's creation (or the last SubmitChanges), and then executes an SQL statement to write them to the database. Any TransactionScope is honored; if none is present, it wraps all statements in a new transaction.

You can also add new or existing rows to an EntitySet by calling Add. LINQ to SQL automatically populates the foreign keys when you do this:

```
var p1 = new Purchase { ID=100, Description="Bike",
                        Price=500 };
var p2 = new Purchase { ID=101, Description="Tools",
                        Price=100 };

Customer cust = dataContext.Customers.Single
                  (c => c.ID == 1);
```

```
cust.Purchases.Add (p1);
cust.Purchases.Remove (p2);

dataContext.SubmitChanges();  // Inserts the purchases
```

NOTE

If you don't want the burden of allocating unique keys,
you can use either an auto-incrementing field (IDENTI-
TY in SQL Server) or a Guid for the primary key.

In this example, LINQ to SQL automatically writes 100 into
the CustomerID column of each of the new purchases. (It
knows to do this because of the association that we defined
on the Purchases property):

```
[Association (Storage="_Purchases",
              OtherKey="CustomerID")]
public EntitySet <Purchase> Purchases
{ get {...} set {...} }
```

If the Customer and Purchase entities were generated by the
Visual Studio designer or SqlMetal, the generated classes
would include further code to keep the two sides of each
relationship in sync. In other words, assigning the Purchase.
Customer property would automatically add the new customer to the Customer.Purchases entity set—and vice versa.
We can illustrate this by rewriting the preceding example as
follows:

```
var dataContext = new MyTypedDataContext ("...");

Customer cust = dataContext.Customers.Single
                (c => c.ID == 1);
new Purchase { ID=100, Description="Bike",  Price=500,
               Customer=cust };
new Purchase { ID=101, Description="Tools", Price=100,
               Customer=cust };

dataContext.SubmitChanges();   // Inserts the purchases
```

When you remove a row from an EntitySet, its foreign key
field is automatically set to null. The following disassociates
our two recently added purchases from their customer:

```
var dataContext = new MyTypedDataContext ("...");

Customer cust = dataContext.Customers.Single
                (c => c.ID == 1);

cust.Purchases.Remove
  (cust.Purchases.Single (p => p.ID == 100));
cust.Purchases.Remove
  (cust.Purchases.Single (p => p.ID == 101));

dataContext.SubmitChanges(); // Submit SQL to server
```

Because this tries to set each purchase's CustomerID field to null, Purchase.CustomerID must be nullable in the database—otherwise, an exception is thrown. (Further, the CustomerID field or property in the entity class must be a nullable type.)

To delete child entities entirely, remove them from the Table<> instead:

```
Customer cust = dataContext.Customers.Single
                (c => c.ID == 1);

var dc = dataContext;
dc.Purchases.DeleteOnSubmit
  (dc.Purchases.Single (p => p.ID == 100));
dc.Purchases.DeleteOnSubmit
  (dc.Purchases.Single (p => p.ID == 101));

dataContext.SubmitChanges(); // Submit SQL to server
```

Building Query Expressions

So far, when we've needed to dynamically compose queries, we've done so by conditionally chaining query operators. Although this is adequate in many scenarios, sometimes you need to work at a more granular level and dynamically compose the lambda expressions that feed the operators.

In this section, we'll assume the following Product class:

```
[Table] public partial class Product
{
  [Column(IsPrimaryKey=true)] public int ID;
  [Column]                    public string Description;
```

```
    [Column]                    public bool Discontinued;
    [Column]                    public DateTime LastSale;
}
```

Delegates Versus Expression Trees

Recall that:

- Local queries, which use `Enumerable` operators, take delegates.
- Interpreted queries, which use `Queryable` operators, take expression trees.

We can see this by comparing the signature of the `Where` operator in `Enumerable` and `Queryable`:

```
public static IEnumerable<TSource> Where<TSource> (this
  IEnumerable<TSource> source,
  Func<TSource,bool> predicate)

public static IQueryable<TSource> Where<TSource> (this
  IQueryable<TSource> source,
  Expression<Func<TSource,bool>> predicate)
```

When embedded within a query, a lambda expression looks identical whether it binds to `Enumerable`'s operators or `Queryable`'s operators:

```
IEnumerable<Product> q1 = localProducts.Where
                          (p => !p.Discontinued);
IQueryable<Product>  q2 = sqlProducts.Where
                          (p => !p.Discontinued);
```

When you assign a lambda expression to an intermediate variable, however, you must be explicit about whether to resolve to a delegate (i.e., `Func<>`) or an expression tree (i.e., `Expression<Func<>>`).

Compiling expression trees

You can convert an expression tree to a delegate by calling `Compile`. This is of particular value when writing methods that return reusable expressions. To illustrate, we'll add a static method to the `Product` class that returns a predicate evaluating to true if a product is not discontinued, and has sold in the past 30 days:

```
public partial class Product
{
  public static Expression<Func<Product, bool>>
  IsSelling()
  {
    return p => !p.Discontinued &&
                p.LastSale > DateTime.Now.AddDays (-30);
  }
}
```

(We've defined this in a separate partial class to avoid being overwritten by an automatic DataContext generator such as Visual Studio's LINQ to SQL designer.)

The method just written can be used both in interpreted and in local queries as follows:

```
void Test()
{
  var dataContext = new MyTypedDataContext ("...");
  Product[] localProducts =
    dataContext.Products.ToArray();

  IQueryable<Product> sqlQuery =
    dataContext.Products.Where (Product.IsSelling());

  IEnumerable<Product> localQuery =
    localProducts.Where (Product.IsSelling.Compile());
}
```

NOTE

You cannot convert in the reverse direction, from a delegate to an expression tree. This makes expression trees more versatile.

AsQueryable

The AsQueryable operator lets you write whole *queries* that can run over either local or remote sequences:

```
IQueryable<Product> FilterSortProducts
  (IQueryable<Product> input)
{
   return from p in input
          where ...
          order by ...
          select p;
}

void Test()
{
  var dataContext = new MyTypedDataContext ("...");
  Product[] localProducts =
    dataContext.Products.ToArray();

  var sqlQuery =
    FilterSortProducts (dataContext.Products);
  var localQuery =
    FilterSortProducts (localProducts.AsQueryable());
  ...
}
```

AsQueryable wraps IQueryable<> clothing around a local
sequence so that subsequent query operators resolve to
expression trees. When you later enumerate over the result,
the expression trees are implicitly compiled, and the local
sequence enumerates as it would ordinarily.

Expression Trees

We said previously that assigning a lambda expression to a
variable of type Expression<TDelegate> causes the C# compiler to emit an expression tree. With some programming
effort, you can do the same thing manually at runtime—in
other words, dynamically build an expression tree from
scratch. The result can be cast to an Expression<TDelegate>
and used in LINQ to SQL queries—or compiled into an ordinary delegate by calling Compile.

The Expression DOM

An expression tree is a miniature code DOM. Each node in the tree is represented by a type in the System.Linq. Expressions namespace; these types are illustrated in Figure 8.

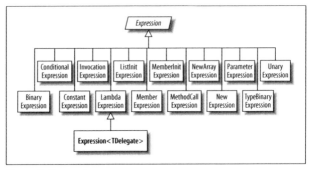

Figure 8. Expression types

The base class for all nodes is the (nongeneric) Expression class. The generic Expression<TDelegate> class actually means "typed lambda expression" and might have been named LambdaExpression<TDelegate> if it weren't for the clumsiness of this:

```
LambdaExpression<Func<Customer,bool>> f = ...
```

Expression<>'s base type is the (nongeneric) LambdaExpression class. LamdbaExpression provides type unification for lambda expression trees: any typed Expression<> can be cast to a LambdaExpression.

The fact that LambdaExpressions have *parameters* distinguishes them from ordinary Expressions. To create an expression tree, you don't instantiate node types directly; rather, you call static methods provided on the Expression class. Here are all the methods:

Add	MakeMemberAccess
AddChecked	MakeUnary
And	MemberBind
AndAlso	MemberInit
ArrayIndex	Modulo
ArrayLength	Multiply
Bind	MultiplyChecked
Call	Negate
Coalesce	NegateChecked
Condition	New
Constant	NewArrayBounds
Convert	NewArrayInit
ConvertChecked	Not
Divide	NotEqual
ElementInit	Or
Equal	OrElse
ExclusiveOr	Parameter
Field	Power
GreaterThan	Property
GreaterThanOrEqual	PropertyOrField
Invoke	Quote
Lambda	RightShift
LeftShift	Subtract
LessThan	SubtractChecked
LessThanOrEqual	TypeAs
ListBind	TypeIs
ListInit	UnaryPlus
MakeBinary	

Figure 9 shows the expression tree that the following assignment creates:

```
Expression<Func<string, bool>> f = s => s.Length < 5;
```

We can demonstrate this as follows:

```
Console.WriteLine (f.Body.NodeType);        // LessThan
Console.WriteLine
  (((BinaryExpression) f.Body).Right);      // 5
```

Let's now build this expression from scratch. The principle is that you start from the bottom of the tree and work your way up. The bottommost thing in our tree is a ParameterExpression, the lambda expression parameter called "s" of type string:

```
ParameterExpression p = Expression.Parameter
  (typeof (string), "s");
```

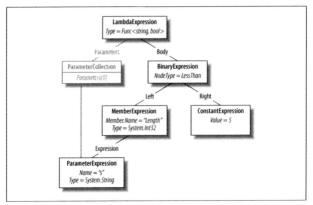

Figure 9. Expression tree

The next step is to build the MemberExpression and
ConstantExpression. In the former case, we need to access
the Length *property* of our parameter, "s":

```
MemberExpression stringLength =
  Expression.Property (p, "Length");
ConstantExpression five = Expression.Constant (5);
```

Next is the LessThan comparison:

```
BinaryExpression comparison =
  Expression.LessThan (stringLength, five);
```

The final step is to construct the lambda expression, which
links an expression Body to a collection of parameters:

```
Expression<Func<string, bool>> lambda =
  Expression.Lambda<Func<string, bool>> (comparison, p);
```

A convenient way to test our lambda is to compile it to a
delegate:

```
Func<string, bool> runnable = lambda.Compile();

Console.WriteLine (runnable ("kangaroo"));    // False
Console.WriteLine (runnable ("dog"));         // True
```

A discussion on dynamically building expression predicates is available online at *www.albahari.com/expressions/*.

Query Operator Overview

The sections that follow describe each of the LINQ query operators, as summarized in Table 1.

Table 1. LINQ query operators

Category	Operators
Filtering	Where, Distinct, Take, TakeWhile, Skip, SkipWhile
Projecting	Select, SelectMany
Joining	Join, GroupJoin
Ordering	OrderBy, OrderByDescending, ThenBy, ThenByDescending, Reverse
Grouping	GroupBy
Set	Concat, Union, Intersect, Except
Conversion (import)	OfType, Cast
Conversion (export)	ToArray, ToList, ToDictionary, ToLookup, AsEnumerable, AsQueryable
Element	First, FirstOrDefault, Last, LastOrDefault, Single, SingleOrDefault, ElementAt, ElementAtOrDefault, DefaultIfEmpty

Table 1. LINQ query operators (continued)

Category	Operators
Aggregation	Aggregate, Average, Count, LongCount, Sum, Max, Min
Quantifiers	All, Any, Contains, SequenceEqual
Generation	Empty, Range, Repeat

The examples assume that a names array is defined as follows:

```
string[] names = { "Tom","Dick","Harry","Mary","Jay" };
```

Examples that use LINQ to SQL assume a typed DataContext variable called dataContext:

```
var dataContext = new DemoDataContext( );

...

public class DemoDataContext : DataContext
{
  public DemoDataContext (string cxString)
    : base (cxString) { }

  public Table<Customer> Customers
  { get { return GetTable<Customer>( ); } }

  public Table<Purchase> Purchases
  { get { return GetTable<Purchase>( ); } }
}

[Table] public class Customer
{
  [Column(IsPrimaryKey=true)] public int ID;
  [Column] public string Name;

  [Association (OtherKey="CustomerID")]
  public EntitySet<Purchase> Purchases
    = new EntitySet<Purchase>( );
}
```

```
[Table] public class Purchase
{
    [Column(IsPrimaryKey=true)] public int ID;
    [Column] public int? CustomerID;
    [Column] public string Description;
    [Column] public decimal Price;
    [Column] public DateTime Date;

  EntityRef<Customer> custRef;

  [Association (Storage="custRef",
               ThisKey="CustomerID",
               IsForeignKey=true)]
  public Customer Customer
  {
    get { return custRef.Entity; }
    set { custRef.Entity = value; }
  }
}
```

NOTE

The LINQ to SQL entity classes shown are a simplified version of what automated tools typically produce, and they do not include code to update the opposing side in a relationship when their entities have been reassigned.

Here are their corresponding SQL table definitions:

```
create table Customer
(
  ID int not null primary key,
  Name varchar(30) not null
)
create table Purchase
(
  ID int not null primary key,
  CustomerID int references Customer (ID),
  Description varchar(30) not null,
  Price decimal not null
)
```

Filtering

Method	Description	SQL equivalents
Where	Returns a subset of elements that satisfy a given condition	WHERE
Take	Returns the first count elements, and discards the rest	WHERE ROW_NUMBER()... *or* TOP *n* subquery
Skip	Ignores the first count elements, and returns the rest	WHERE ROW_NUMBER()... *or* NOT IN (SELECT TOP *n*...)
TakeWhile	Emits elements from the input sequence until the predicate is true	Exception thrown
SkipWhile	Ignores elements from the input sequence until the predicate is true, and then emits the rest	Exception thrown
Distinct	Returns a collection that excludes duplicates	SELECT DISTINCT...

NOTE

The "SQL equivalents" column in the reference tables does not necessarily correspond to what an IQueryable implementation such as LINQ to SQL will produce. Rather, it indicates what you'd typically use to do the same job if you were writing the SQL query yourself. Where there is no simple translation, the column is left blank. Where there is no translation at all, the column reads "Exception thrown."

Enumerable implementation code, when shown, excludes checking for null arguments, and indexing predicates.

With each of the filtering methods, you always end up with either the same number or fewer elements than you started with. You can never get more! The elements are also identical when they come out; they are not transformed in any way.

Where

Argument	Type
Source sequence	IEnumerable<TSource>
Predicate	TSource => bool or (TSource,int) => bool*

*Prohibited with LINQ to SQL

Comprehension syntax

```
where bool-expression
```

Overview

Where returns the elements from the input sequence that satisfy the given predicate.

For instance:

```
string[] names = { "Tom","Dick","Harry","Mary","Jay" };
IEnumerable<string> query =
  names.Where (name => name.EndsWith ("y"));

// Result: { "Harry", "Mary", "Jay" }
```

In comprehension syntax:

```
IEnumerable<string> query = from n in names
                            where n.EndsWith ("y")
                            select n;
```

A where clause can appear more than once in a query, and it can be interspersed with let clauses:

```
from n in names
where n.Length > 3
let u = n.ToUpper( )
where u.EndsWith ("Y")
select u;                    // Result: { "HARRY", "MARY" }
```

Standard C# scoping rules apply to such queries. In other words, you cannot refer to a variable prior to declaring it with an iteration variable or a let clause.

Indexed filtering

Where's predicate optionally accepts a second argument of type int. This is fed with the position of each element within the input sequence, allowing the predicate to use this information in its filtering decision. For example, the following skips every second element:

```
IEnumerable<string> query =
  names.Where ((n, i) => i % 2 == 0);

// Result: { "Tom", "Harry", "Jay" }
```

An exception is thrown if you use indexed filtering in LINQ to SQL.

Where in LINQ to SQL

The following methods on string translate to SQL's LIKE operator:

```
Contains, StartsWith, EndsWith
```

For instance, c.Name.Contains ("abc") translates to customer.Name LIKE '%abc%' (or more accurately, a parameterized version of this). You can perform more complex comparisons by calling SqlMethods.Like; this method maps directly to SQL's LIKE operator. You can also perform *order* comparison on strings with string's CompareTo method; this maps to SQL's < and > operators:

```
dataContext.Purchases.Where (p => p.Description.CompareTo
("C") < 0)
```

LINQ to SQL also allows you to apply the Contains operator to a local collection within a filter predicate. For instance:

```
string[] chosenOnes = { "Tom", "Jay" };

from c in dataContext.Customers
where chosenOnes.Contains (c.Name)
...
```

This maps to SQL's IN operator—in other words:

```
WHERE customer.Name IN ("Tom", "Jay")
```

If the local collection is an array of entities or nonscalar types, LINQ to SQL may instead emit an EXISTS clause.

Take and Skip

Argument	Type
Source sequence	IEnumerable<TSource>
Number of elements to take or skip	int

Take emits the first *n* elements and discards the rest; Skip discards the first *n* elements and emits the rest. The two methods are useful together when implementing a web page, allowing a user to navigate through a large set of matching records. For instance, suppose a user searches a book database for the term "mercury" and there are 100 matches. The following returns the first 20:

```
IQueryable<Book> query = dataContext.Books
  .Where    (b => b.Title.Contains ("mercury"))
  .OrderBy  (b => b.Title)
  .Take (20);
```

The next query returns books 21 to 40:

```
IQueryable<Book> query = dataContext.Books
  .Where    (b => b.Title.Contains ("mercury"))
  .OrderBy  (b => b.Title)
  .Skip (20).Take (20);
```

LINQ to SQL translates Take and Skip to the ROW_NUMBER function in SQL Server 2005, or a TOP *n* subquery in earlier versions of SQL Server.

TakeWhile and SkipWhile

Argument	Type
Source sequence	IEnumerable<TSource>
Predicate	TSource => bool or (TSource, int) => bool

TakeWhile enumerates the input sequence, emitting each item until the given predicate is true. It then ignores the remaining elements:

```
int[] numbers       = { 3, 5, 2, 234, 4, 1 };
var takeWhileSmall = numbers.TakeWhile (n => n < 100);

// RESULT: { 3, 5, 2 }
```

SkipWhile enumerates the input sequence, ignoring each item until the given predicate is true. It then emits the remaining elements:

```
int[] numbers       = { 3, 5, 2, 234, 4, 1 };
var skipWhileSmall = numbers.SkipWhile (n => n < 100);

// RESULT: { 234, 4, 1 }
```

TakeWhile and SkipWhile have no translation to SQL, and they cause a runtime error if used in a LINQ to SQL query.

Distinct

Distinct returns the input sequence stripped of duplicates. Only the default equality comparer can be used for equality comparison. The following returns distinct letters in a string:

```
char[] distinctLetters =
  "HelloWorld".Distinct().ToArray();
string s = new string (distinctLetters);    // HeloWrd
```

We can call LINQ methods directly on a string because string implements IEnumerable<char>.

Projecting

Method	Description	SQL equivalents
Select	Transforms each input element with the given lambda expression	SELECT
SelectMany	Transforms each input element, then flattens and concatenates the resultant subsequences	INNER JOIN, LEFT OUTER JOIN, CROSS JOIN

Select

Argument	Type
Source sequence	IEnumerable<TSource>
Result selector	TSource => TResult or (TSource, int) => TResult[a]

[a] Prohibited with LINQ to SQL

*Comprehension syntax

```
select projection-expression
```

Overview

With Select, you always get the same number of elements that you started with. Each element, however, can be transformed in any manner by the lambda function.

The following selects the names of all fonts installed on the computer (from System.Drawing):

```
IEnumerable<string> query =
  from f in FontFamily.Families
  select f.Name;

foreach (string name in query) Console.WriteLine (name);
```

In this example, the select clause converts a FontFamily object to its name. Here's the lambda equivalent:

```
IEnumerable<string> query =
  FontFamily.Families.Select (f => f.Name);
```

Select statements are often used to project into anonymous types:

```
var query =
  from f in FontFamily.Families
  select new
  {
    f.Name,
    LineSpacing = f.GetLineSpacing (FontStyle.Bold)
  };
```

A projection with no transformation is sometimes used in comprehension queries to satisfy the requirement that the query end in a select or group clause. The following selects fonts supporting strikeout:

```
IEnumerable<FontFamily> query =
  from f in FontFamily.Families
  where f.IsStyleAvailable (FontStyle.Strikeout)
  select f;

foreach (FontFamily ff in query)
  Console.WriteLine (ff.Name);
```

In such cases, the compiler omits the projection when translating to lambda syntax.

Indexed projection

The selector expression can optionally accept an integer argument, which acts as an indexer, providing the expression with the position of each input in the input sequence. This works only with local queries:

```
string[] names = { "Tom","Dick","Harry","Mary","Jay" };

IEnumerable<string> query = names
  .Select ((s,i) => i + "=" + s);

// RESULT: { "0=Tom", "1=Dick", "2=Harry", ... }
```

Select subqueries and object hierarchies

You can nest a subquery in a select clause to build an object hierarchy. The following example returns a collection describing each directory under *D:\source*, with a subcollection of files under each directory:

```
DirectoryInfo[] dirs =
  new DirectoryInfo (@"d:\source").GetDirectories();

var query =
  from d in dirs
  where (d.Attributes & FileAttributes.System) == 0
  select new
  {
    DirectoryName = d.FullName,
    Created = d.CreationTime,
    Files =
      from f in d.GetFiles()
      where (f.Attributes & FileAttributes.Hidden) == 0
      select new { FileName = f.Name, f.Length, }
  };
```

The inner portion of this query can be called a *correlated subquery*. A subquery is correlated if it references an object in the outer query—in this case, it references d, the directory being enumerated.

NOTE

A subquery inside a Select allows you to map one object hierarchy to another or map a relational object model to a hierarchical object model.

With local queries, a subquery within a Select causes double-deferred execution. In our example, the files don't get filtered or projected until the inner foreach statement enumerates.

Subqueries and joins in LINQ to SQL

Subquery projections work well in LINQ to SQL, and they can be used to do the work of SQL-style joins. Here's how we retrieve each customer's name along with his high-value purchases:

```
var query =
  from c in dataContext.Customers
  select new
  {
```

```
      c.Name,
      Purchases =
        from p in dataContext.Purchases
        where p.CustomerID == c.ID && p.Price > 1000
        select new { p.Description, p.Price }
    };
```

NOTE

This style of query is ideally suited to interpreted queries.
LINQ to SQL processes the outer query and subquery as
a unit, avoiding unnecessary round-tripping. With local
queries, however, it's inefficient because every combination of outer and inner element must be enumerated to
get the few matching combinations. A better choice for
local queries is `Join` or `GroupJoin`, described in the following sections.

This query matches up objects from two disparate collections, and can be thought of as a "join." The difference
between this and a conventional database join (or subquery)
is that we're not flattening the output into a single two-
dimensional result set. We're mapping the relational data to
hierarchical data rather than to flat data.

Here's the same query simplified using the `Purchases` association property on the `Customer` entity:

```
from c in dataContext.Customers
select new
{
  c.Name,
  Purchases = from p in c.Purchases
              where p.Price > 1000
              select new { p.Description, p.Price }
};
```

Both queries are analogous to a left outer join in SQL in the
sense that we get all customers in the outer enumeration,
regardless of whether they have any purchases. To emulate
an inner join—where customers without high-value purchases are excluded—we would need to add a filter condition on the purchases collection:

```
from c in dataContext.Customers
where c.Purchases.Any (p => p.Price > 1000)
select new {
                c.Name,
                Purchases =
                  from p in c.Purchases
                  where p.Price > 1000
                  select new { p.Description, p.Price }
            };
```

This is slightly untidy, however, in that we've written the same predicate (Price > 1000) twice. We can avoid this duplication with a let clause:

```
from c in dataContext.Customers
let highValueP = from p in c.Purchases
                 where p.Price > 1000
                 select new { p.Description, p.Price }
where highValueP.Any()
select new { c.Name, Purchases = highValueP };
```

This style of query is flexible. By changing Any to Count, for instance, we can modify the query to retrieve only customers with at least two high-value purchases:

```
...
where highValueP.Count() >= 2
select new { c.Name, Purchases = highValueP };
```

Projecting into concrete types

Projecting into anonymous types is useful in obtaining intermediate results, but not so useful if you want to send a result set back to a client, for instance, because anonymous types can exist only as local variables within a method. An alternative is to use concrete types for projections, such as DataSets or custom business entity classes. A custom business entity is simply a class that you write with some properties, similar to a LINQ to SQL [Table] annotated class, but designed to hide lower-level (database-related) details. You might exclude foreign key fields from business entity classes, for instance. Assuming we wrote custom entity classes called CustomerEntity and PurchaseEntity, here's how we could project into them:

```
IQueryable<CustomerEntity> query =
  from c in dataContext.Customers
  select new CustomerEntity
  {
    Name = c.Name,
    Purchases = (
      from p in c.Purchases
      where p.Price > 1000
      select new PurchaseEntity
      {
        Description = p.Description,
        Value = p.Price
      }
    ).ToList()
  };

// Force query execution, converting output to a
// more convenient List:
List<CustomerEntity> result = query.ToList();
```

Notice that so far, we've not had to use a Join or SelectMany statement. This is because we're maintaining the hierarchical shape of the data, as illustrated in Figure 10. With LINQ, you can often avoid the traditional SQL approach of flattening tables into a two-dimensional result set.

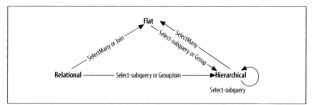

Figure 10. Projecting an object hierarchy

SelectMany

Argument	Type
Source sequence	IEnumerable<TSource>
Result selector	TSource => IEnumerable<TResult> or (TSource,int) => IEnumerable<TResult>[a]

[a] Prohibited with LINQ to SQL

Comprehension syntax

```
from identifier1 in enumerable-expression1
from identifier2 in enumerable-expression2
```

Overview

SelectMany concatenates subsequences into a single flat output sequence.

Recall that for each input element, Select yields exactly one output element. In contrast, SelectMany yields *0..n* output elements. The *0..n* elements come from a subsequence or child sequence that the lambda expression must emit.

SelectMany can be used to expand child sequences, flatten nested collections, and join two collections into a flat output sequence. Using the conveyer belt analogy, SelectMany funnels fresh material onto a conveyer belt. With SelectMany, each input element is the *trigger* for the introduction of fresh material. The fresh material is emitted by the selector lambda expression, and it must be a sequence. In other words, the lambda expression must emit a *child sequence* per input *element*. The final result is a concatenation of the child sequences emitted for each input element.

Let's start with a simple example. Suppose we have an array of names as follows:

```
string[] fullNames =
  { "Anne Williams", "John Fred Smith", "Sue Green" };
```

that we wish to convert to a single flat collection of words—in other words:

```
"Anne","Williams","John","Fred","Smith","Sue",Green"
```

SelectMany is ideal for this task because we're mapping each input element to a variable number of output elements. All we must do is come up with a selector expression that converts each input element to a child sequence. string.Split does the job nicely: it takes a string and splits it into words, emitting the result as an array:

```
string testInputElement = "Anne Williams";
string[] childSequence = testInputElement.Split();

// childSequence is { "Anne", "Williams" };
```

So, here's our SelectMany query and the result:

```
IEnumerable<string> query =
  fullNames.SelectMany (name => name.Split());

foreach (string name in query)
  Console.Write (name + "|");

// RESULT: Anne|Williams|John|Fred|Smith|Sue|Green|
```

NOTE

If you replace SelectMany with Select, you get the same results in hierarchical form. The following emits a sequence of string *arrays*, requiring nested foreach statements to enumerate:

```
IEnumerable<string[]> query =
  fullNames.Select (
    name => name.Split());

foreach (string[] stringArray in query)
  foreach (string name in stringArray)
    Console.Write (name + "/");
```

The benefit of SelectMany is that it yields a single *flat* result sequence.

SelectMany is supported in query comprehension syntax and is invoked by having an *additional generator*—in other words, an extra from clause in the query. The from keyword has two meanings in comprehension syntax. At the start of a query, it introduces the original iteration variable and input sequence. *Anywhere else* in the query, it translates to SelectMany. Here's our query in comprehension syntax:

```
IEnumerable<string> query =
  from fullName in fullNames
  from name in fullName.Split()
  select name;
```

Note that the additional generator introduces a new query variable—in this case, name. The new query variable becomes the iteration variable from then on, and the old iteration variable is demoted to an *outer iteration variable*.

Outer iteration variables

In the preceding example, fullName becomes an outer iteration variable after the SelectMany. Outer iteration variables remain in scope until the query either ends or reaches an into clause. The extended scope of these variables is *the* killer scenario for comprehension syntax over lambda syntax.

To illustrate, we can take the preceding query and include fullName in the final projection:

```
IEnumerable<string> query =
  from fullName in fullNames        // outer variable
  from name in fullName.Split( )    // iteration variable
  select name + " came from " + fullName;

Anne came from Anne Williams
Williams came from Anne Williams
John came from John Fred Smith
...
```

Behind the scenes, the compiler must pull some tricks to resolve outer references. A good way to appreciate this is to try writing the same query in lambda syntax. It's tricky! It gets harder still if you insert a where or orderby clause before projecting:

```
from fullName in fullNames
from name in fullName.Split( )
orderby fullName, name
select name + " came from " + fullName;
```

The problem is that SelectMany emits a flat sequence of child elements—in our case, a flat collection of words. The original outer element from which it came (fullName) is lost. The solution is to "carry" the outer element with each child in a temporary anonymous type:

```
from fullName in fullNames
from x in
  fullName.Split()
          .Select (name => new { name, fullName } )
orderby x.fullName, x.name
select x.name + " came from " + x.fullName;
```

The only change here is that we're wrapping each child element (name) in an anonymous type that also contains its fullName. This is similar to how a let clause is resolved. Here's the final conversion to lambda syntax:

```
IEnumerable<string> query = fullNames
  .SelectMany (fName =>
    fName.Split()
          .Select (name => new { name, fName } ))
  .OrderBy (x => x.fName)
  .ThenBy  (x => x.name)
  .Select  (x => x.name + " came from " + x.fName);
```

NOTE

SelectMany provides an overload that performs a SelectMany and Select in one step. We could use this to (slightly) simplify the preceding example, replacing the code in boldface with this:

```
.SelectMany (
  fName => fName.Split(),
  (fName, name) => new { name, fName }
)
```

Thinking in comprehension syntax

As we just demonstrated, there are good reasons to use comprehension syntax if you need the outer iteration variable. In such cases, it helps not only to use comprehension syntax, but also to think directly in its terms.

There are two basic patterns when writing additional generators. The first is expanding and flattening subsequences. To do this, call a property or method on an existing query variable in your additional generator. We did this in the previous example:

```
from fullName in fullNames
from name in fullName.Split()
```

Here, we've expanded from enumerating full names to enumerating words. An analogous query in LINQ to SQL is when you expand child association properties. The following query lists all customers along with their purchases:

```
IEnumerable<string> query =
  from c in dataContext.Customers
  from p in c.Purchases
  select c.Name + " bought a " + p.Description;

Tom bought a Bike
Tom bought a Holiday
Dick bought a Phone
Harry bought a Car
...
```

Here, we've expanded each customer into a subsequence of purchases.

The second pattern is performing a *cross product* or *cross join*—where every element of one sequence is matched with every element of another. To do this, you introduce a generator whose selector expression returns a sequence unrelated to an iteration variable:

```
int[] numbers = { 1, 2, 3 };
string[] letters = { "a", "b" };

IEnumerable<string> query = from n in numbers
                           from l in letters
                           select n.ToString() + l;

RESULT: { "1a", "1b", "2a", "2b", "3a", "3b" }
```

This style of query is the basis of SelectMany-style *joins*.

Joining with SelectMany

You can use SelectMany to join two sequences simply by filtering the results of a cross product. For instance, suppose we wanted to match players for a game. We could start as follows:

```
string[] players = { "Tom", "Jay", "Mary" };

IEnumerable<string> query =
  from name1 in players
  from name2 in players
  select name1 + " vs " + name2;
```

```
RESULT: {"Tom vs Tom", "Tom vs Jay", "Tom vs Mary",
         "Jay vs Tom", "Jay vs Jay", "Jay vs Mary",
         "Mary vs Tom", "Mary vs "Jay", "Mary vs Mary"}
```

The query reads: "For every player, reiterate every player, selecting player 1 versus player 2." Although we got what we asked for (a cross join), the results are not useful until we add a filter:

```
IEnumerable<string> query =
  from name1 in players
  from name2 in players
  where name1.CompareTo (name2) < 0
  orderby name1, name2
  select name1 + " vs " + name2;
```

```
RESULT: { "Jay vs Mary", "Jay vs Tom", "Mary vs Tom" }
```

The filter predicate constitutes the *join condition*. Our query can be called a *non-equi join* because the join condition doesn't use an equality operator. We'll demonstrate the remaining types of joins with LINQ to SQL.

SelectMany in LINQ to SQL

SelectMany in LINQ to SQL can perform cross joins, non-equi joins, inner joins, and left outer joins. You can use SelectMany with both predefined associations and ad hoc relationships—just as with Select. The difference is that SelectMany returns a flat rather than a hierarchical result set.

A cross join in LINQ to SQL is written just as in the preceding section. The following query matches every customer to every purchase (a cross join):

```
var query =
  from c in dataContext.Customers
  from p in dataContext.Purchases
  select c.Name + " might have bought " + p.Description;
```

More typically, though, you'd want to match customers to their own purchases only. You achieve this by adding a where clause with a joining predicate. This results in a standard SQL-style equi-join:

```
var query =
  from c in dataContext.Customers
  from p in dataContext.Purchases
  where c.ID == p.CustomerID
  select c.Name + " bought a " + p.Description;
```

NOTE

This translates well to SQL. In the next section, we'll see how it extends to support outer joins. Reformulating such queries with LINQ's Join operator actually makes them *less* extensible—LINQ is opposite to SQL in this sense.

If you have association properties for relationships in your LINQ to SQL entities, you can express the same query by expanding the subcollection instead of filtering the cross product:

```
from c in dataContext.Customers
from p in c.Purchases
select new { c.Name, p.Description };
```

The advantage is that we've eliminated the joining predicate. We've gone from filtering a cross product to expanding and flattening it. Both queries, however, will result in the same SQL.

You can add where clauses to such a query for additional filtering. For instance, if we wanted only customers whose names started with J, we could filter as follows:

```
from c in dataContext.Customers
where c.Name.StartsWith ("J")
from p in c.Purchases
select new { c.Name, p.Description };
```

This LINQ to SQL query would work equally well if the where clause was moved one line down. If it were a local query, however, moving the where clause down would make it less efficient. With local queries, you should filter *before* joining.

You can introduce new tables into the mix with additional from clauses. For instance, if each purchase had purchase item child rows, you could produce a flat result set of customers with their purchases, each with their purchase detail lines as follows:

```
from c in dataContext.Customers
from p in c.Purchases
from pi in p.PurchaseItems
select new { c.Name, p.Description, pi.DetailLine };
```

Each from clause introduces a new *child* table. To include data from a *parent* table (via an association property), you don't add a from clause; you simply navigate to the property. For example, if each customer had a salesperson whose name you wanted to query, you'd just do this:

```
from c in dataContext.Customers
select new {
            Name = c.Name,
            SalesPerson = c.SalesPerson.Name
          };
```

You don't use SelectMany in this case because there's no subcollection to flatten. Parent association properties return a single item.

Outer joins with SelectMany

We saw previously that a Select-subquery yields a result analogous to a left outer join:

```
from c in dataContext.Customers
select new {
            c.Name,
            Purchases =
              from p in c.Purchases
              where p.Price > 1000
              select new { p.Description, p.Price }
          };
```

In this example, every outer element (customer) is included, regardless of whether the customer has any purchases. But suppose we rewrite this query with `SelectMany`, so we can obtain a single flat collection rather than a hierarchical result set:

```
from c in dataContext.Customers
from p in c.Purchases
where p.Price > 1000
select new { c.Name, p.Description, p.Price };
```

In the process of flattening the query, we've switched to an inner join; customers are now included only for whom one or more high-value purchases exists. To get a left outer join with a flat result set, we must apply the `DefaultIfEmpty` query operator on the inner sequence. This method returns null if its input sequence has no elements. Here's such a query, price predicate aside:

```
from c in dataContext.Customers
from p in c.Purchases.DefaultIfEmpty()
select new {
            c.Name,
            p.Description,
            Price = (decimal?) p.Price
          };
```

This works perfectly with LINQ to SQL, returning all customers even if they have no purchases. But if we were to run this as a local query, it would crash because when p is null, p.Description and p.Price throw a `NullReferenceException`. We can make our query robust in either scenario as follows:

```
from c in dataContext.Customers
from p in c.Purchases.DefaultIfEmpty()
select new
{
  c.Name,
  Descript = p == null ? null : p.Description,
  Price = p == null ? (decimal?) null : p.Price
};
```

Let's now reintroduce the price filter. We cannot use a where clause as we did before because it would execute *after* DefaultIfEmpty:

```
from c in dataContext.Customers
from p in c.Purchases.DefaultIfEmpty()
where p.Price > 1000...
```

The correct solution is to splice the Where clause *before* DefaultIfEmpty with a subquery:

```
from c in dataContext.Customers
from p in c.Purchases.Where (p => p.Price > 1000)
                     .DefaultIfEmpty()
select new
{
  c.Name,
  Descript = p == null ? null : p.Description,
  Price = p == null ? (decimal?) null : p.Price
};
```

This translates to a left outer join in LINQ to SQL, and it is an effective pattern for writing this type of query.

NOTE

If you're used to writing outer joins in SQL, you might be tempted to overlook the simpler option of a Select-subquery in favor of the awkward but familiar SQL-centric flat approach. The hierarchical result set from a Select-subquery is often better suited to outer join-style queries because there are no additional nulls to deal with.

Joining

Method	Description	SQL equivalents
Join	Applies a lookup strategy to match elements from two collections, emitting a flat result set	INNER JOIN
GroupJoin	As above, but emits a *hierarchical* result set	INNER JOIN, LEFT OUTER JOIN

Join and GroupJoin

Join arguments

Argument	Type
Outer sequence	IEnumerable<TOuter>
Inner sequence	IEnumerable<TInner>
Outer key selector	TOuter => TKey
Inner key selector	TInner => TKey
Result selector	(TOuter,TInner) => TResult

GroupJoin arguments

Argument	Type
Outer sequence	IEnumerable<TOuter>
Inner sequence	IEnumerable<TInner>
Outer key selector	TOuter => TKey
Inner key selector	TInner => TKey
Result selector	(TOuter,**IEnumerable<TInner>**) => Tresult

Return type = IEnumerable<TResult>

Comprehension syntax

```
from outer-var in outer-enumerable
join inner-var in inner-enumerable
  on outer-key-expr equals inner-key-expr
[ into identifier ]
```

Overview

Join and GroupJoin mesh two input sequences into a single output sequence. Join emits flat output; GroupJoin emits hierarchical output.

Join and GroupJoin provide an alternative strategy to Select and SelectMany. The advantage of Join and GroupJoin is that they execute efficiently over local in-memory collections because they first load the inner sequence into a keyed lookup, avoiding the need to repeatedly enumerate over every inner element. Their disadvantage is that they offer the equivalent of inner and left outer joins only; cross joins and non-equi joins must still be done with Select/SelectMany. With LINQ to SQL queries, Join and GroupJoin offer no real benefits over Select and SelectMany.

The differences between each of the joining strategies can be summarized as follows.

Strategy	Result shape	Local query speed	Inner joins	Left outer joins	Cross joins	Non-equi joins
SelectMany	Flat	Slow	Yes	Yes	Yes	Yes
Select + Select	Nested	Slow	Yes	Yes	Yes	Yes
Join	Flat	Fast	Yes	-	-	-
GroupJoin	Nested	Fast	Yes	Yes	-	-
GroupJoin + SelectMany	Flat	Fast	Yes	Yes	-	-

Join

The Join operator performs an inner join, emitting a flat output sequence.

The simplest way to demonstrate Join is with LINQ to SQL. The following query lists all customers alongside their purchases without using an association property:

```
IQueryable<string> query =
  from c in dataContext.Customers
  join p in dataContext.Purchases
    on c.ID equals p.CustomerID
  select c.Name + " bought a " + p.Description;
```

The results match what we would get from a `SelectMany`-style query:

```
Tom bought a Bike
Tom bought a Holiday
Dick bought a Phone
Harry bought a Car
```

To see the benefit of `Join` over `SelectMany`, we must convert this to a local query. We can demonstrate this by first copying all customers and purchases to arrays, and then querying the arrays:

```
Customer[] customers = dataContext.Customers.ToArray();
Purchase[] purchases = dataContext.Purchases.ToArray();

var slowQuery =
  from c in customers
  from p in purchases where c.ID == p.CustomerID
  select c.Name + " bought a " + p.Description;

var fastQuery =
  from c in customers
  join p in purchases on c.ID equals p.CustomerID
  select c.Name + " bought a " + p.Description;
```

Although both queries yield the same results, the `Join` query is considerably faster because its implementation in `Enumerable` preloads the inner collection (`purchases`) into a keyed lookup.

The comprehension syntax for `join` can be written in general terms as follows:

```
join inner-var in inner-sequence
on outer-key-expr equals inner-key-expr
```

Join operators in LINQ differentiate between the *outer sequence* and *inner sequence*. Syntactically:

- The *outer sequence* is the input sequence (in this case, `customers`).
- The *inner sequence* is the new collection you introduce (in this case, `purchases`).

Join performs inner joins, meaning customers without purchases are excluded from the output. With inner joins, you can swap the inner and outer sequences in the query and still get the same results:

```
from p in purchases
join c in customers on p.CustomerID equals c.ID
...
```

You can add further join clauses to the same query. If each purchase, for instance, had one or more purchase items, you could join them as follows:

```
from c in customers
join p in purchases on c.ID equals p.CustomerID
join pi in purchaseItems on p.ID equals pi.PurchaseID
...
```

purchases acts as the inner sequence in the first join, and the outer sequence in the second join. You could obtain the same results (inefficiently) using nested foreach statements as follows:

```
foreach (Customer c in customers)
  foreach (Purchase p in purchases)
    if (c.ID == p.CustomerID)
      foreach (PurchaseItem pi in purchaseItems)
        if (p.ID == pi.PurchaseID)
          Console.WriteLine (c.Name + "," + p.Price +
                                        "," + pi.Detail);
```

In query comprehension syntax, variables from earlier joins remain in scope—just as outer iteration variables do with SelectMany-style queries. You're also permitted to insert where and let clauses in between join clauses.

Joining on multiple keys

You can join on multiple keys with anonymous types as follows:

```
from x in seqX
join y in seqY on new { K1 = x.Prop1, K2 = x.Prop2 }
          equals new { K1 = y.Prop3, K2 = y.Prop4 }
...
```

For this to work, the two anonymous types must be structured identically. The compiler then implements each with the same internal type, making the joining keys compatible.

Joining in lambda syntax

The following comprehension syntax join:

```
from c in customers
join p in purchases on c.ID equals p.CustomerID
select new { c.Name, p.Description, p.Price };
```

in lambda syntax is as follows:

```
customers.Join (                    // outer collection
      purchases,                    // inner collection
      c => c.ID,                    // outer key selector
      p => p.CustomerID,            // inner key selector
      (c, p) => new                 // result selector
          { c.Name, p.Description, p.Price }
);
```

The result selector expression at the end creates each element in the output sequence. If you have additional clauses prior to projecting, such as orderby in this example:

```
from c in customers
join p in purchases on c.ID equals p.CustomerID
orderby p.Price
select c.Name + " bought a " + p.Description;
```

you must manufacture a temporary anonymous type in the result selector in lambda syntax. This keeps both c and p in scope following the join:

```
customers.Join (                    // outer collection
      purchases,                    // inner collection
      c => c.ID,                    // outer key selector
      p => p.CustomerID,            // inner key selector
      (c, p) => new { c, p } )      // result selector
   .OrderBy (x => x.p.Price)
   .Select  (x => x.c.Name + " bought a "
                            + x.p.Description);
```

Comprehension syntax is usually preferable when joining; it's less fiddly.

GroupJoin

GroupJoin does the same work as Join, but instead of yielding a flat result, it yields a hierarchical result, grouped by each outer element. It also allows left outer joins.

The comprehension syntax for GroupJoin is the same for Join, but it is followed by the into keyword.

Here's the most basic example:

```
IEnumerable<IEnumerable<Purchase>> query =
  from c in customers
  join p in purchases on c.ID equals p.CustomerID
  into custPurchases
  select custPurchases;   // custPurchases is a sequence
```

NOTE

An into clause translates to GroupJoin only when it appears directly after a join clause. After a select or group clause, it means *query continuation*. The two uses of the into keyword are quite different, although they have one feature in common: they both introduce a new query variable.

The result is a sequence of sequences, which we could enumerate as follows:

```
foreach (IEnumerable<Purchase> purchaseSequence in query)
  foreach (Purchase p in purchaseSequence)
    Console.WriteLine (p.Description);
```

This isn't very useful, however, because outerSeq has no reference to the outer customer. More commonly, you'd reference the outer iteration variable in the projection:

```
from c in customers
join p in purchases on c.ID equals p.CustomerID
into custPurchases
select new { CustName = c.Name, custPurchases };
```

This gives the same results as the following (inefficient) Select-subquery:

```
from c in customers
select new
{
  CustName = c.Name,
  custPurchases =
    purchases.Where (p => c.ID == p.CustomerID)
};
```

By default, GroupJoin does the equivalent of a left outer join. To get an inner join—where customers without purchases are excluded—you need to filter on custPurchases:

```
from c in customers join p in purchases
  on c.ID equals p.CustomerID
into custPurchases
where custPurchases.Any( )
select ...
```

Clauses after a group-join into operate on *subsequences* of inner child elements, not *individual* child elements. This means that to filter individual purchases, you'd have to call Where *before* joining:

```
from c in customers
join p in purchases.Where (p2 => p2.Price > 1000)
  on c.ID equals p.CustomerID
into custPurchases ...
```

You can construct lambda queries with GroupJoin as you would with Join.

Flat outer joins

You run into a dilemma if you want both an outer join and a flat result set. GroupJoin gives you the outer join; Join gives you the flat result set. The solution is to first call GroupJoin, and then DefaultIfEmpty on each child sequence, and then finally SelectMany on the result:

```
from c in customers
join p in purchases on c.ID equals p.CustomerID
into custPurchases
from cp in custPurchases.DefaultIfEmpty( )
select new
```

```
{
  CustName = c.Name,
  Price = cp == null ? (decimal?) null : cp.Price
};
```

`DefaultIfEmpty` emits a null value if a subsequence of purchases is empty. The second `from` clause translates to
`SelectMany`. In this role, it *expands and flattens* all the purchase subsequences, concatenating them into a single
sequence of purchase *elements*.

Joining with lookups

The `Join` and `GroupJoin` methods in `Enumerable` work in two
steps. First, they load the inner sequence into a *lookup*. Second, they query the outer sequence in combination with the
lookup.

A lookup is a sequence of groupings that can be accessed
directly by key. Another way to think of it is as a dictionary
of sequences—a dictionary that can accept many elements
under each key. Lookups are read-only and defined by the
following interface:

```
public interface ILookup<TKey,TElement> :
  IEnumerable<IGrouping<TKey,TElement>>, IEnumerable
{
  int Count { get; }
  bool Contains (TKey key);
  IEnumerable<TElement> this [TKey key] { get; }
}
```

NOTE

The joining operators—like other sequence-emitting operators—honor deferred or lazy execution semantics.
This means the lookup is not built until you begin enumerating the output sequence.

You can create and query lookups manually as an alternative
strategy to using the joining operators when dealing with
local collections. This allows you to reuse the same lookup
over multiple queries.

The ToLookupTT extension method creates a lookup. The following loads all purchases into a lookup—keyed by their CustomerID:

```
ILookup<int?,Purchase> purchLookup =
  purchases.ToLookup (p => p.CustomerID, p => p);
```

The first argument selects the key; the second argument selects the objects that are to be loaded as values into the lookup.

Reading a lookup is rather like reading a dictionary, except that the indexer returns a *sequence* of matching items, rather than a *single* matching item. The following enumerates all purchases made by the customer whose ID is 1:

```
foreach (Purchase p in purchLookup [1])
  Console.WriteLine (p.Description);
```

With a lookup in place, you can write SelectMany/Select queries that execute as efficiently as Join/GroupJoin queries. Join is equivalent to using SelectMany on a lookup:

```
from c in customers
from p in purchLookup [c.ID]
select new { c.Name, p.Description, p.Price };

Tom Bike 500
Tom Holiday 2000
Dick Bike 600
Dick Phone 300
...
```

Adding a call to DefaultIfEmpty makes this into an outer join:

```
from c in customers
from p in purchLookup [c.ID].DefaultIfEmpty()
select new
{
  c.Name,
  Descript = p == null ? null : p.Description,
  Price = p == null ? (decimal?) null : p.Price
};
```

GroupJoin is equivalent to a reading the lookup inside a projection:

```
from c in customers
select new {
          CustName = c.Name,
          CustPurchases = purchLookup [c.ID]
        };
```

Ordering

Method	Description	SQL equivalents
OrderBy, ThenBy	Sorts a sequence in ascending order	ORDER BY ...
OrderByDescending, ThenByDescending	Sorts a sequence in descending order	ORDER BY ... DESC
Reverse	Returns a sequence in reverse order	Exception thrown

Ordering operators return the same elements in a different order.

OrderBy, OrderByDescending, ThenBy, ThenByDescending

OrderBy, OrderByDescending arguments

Argument	Type
Input sequence	IEnumerable<TSource>
Key selector	TSource => TKey

Return type = IOrderedEnumerable<TSource>

ThenBy, ThenByDescending arguments

Argument	Type
Input sequence	IOrderedEnumerable<TSource>
Key selector	TSource => TKey

Comprehension syntax

```
orderby expression1 [descending]
  [, expression2 [descending] ... ]
```

Overview

OrderBy returns a sorted version of the input sequence, using the keySelector expression to make comparisons. The following query emits a sequence of names in alphabetical order:

```
IEnumerable<string> query = names.OrderBy (s => s);
```

The following sorts names by length:

```
IEnumerable<string> query =
  names.OrderBy (s => s.Length);

// Result: { "Jay", "Tom", "Mary", "Dick", "Harry" };
```

The relative order of elements with the same sorting key (in this case, Jay/Tom and Mary/Dick) is indeterminate—unless you append a ThenBy operator:

```
IEnumerable<string> query = names.OrderBy (s => s.Length)
                                 .ThenBy (s => s);

// Result: { "Jay", "Tom", "Dick", "Mary", "Harry" };
```

ThenBy reorders only elements that had the same sorting key in the preceding sort. You can chain any number of ThenBy operators. The following sorts first by length, then by the second character, and finally by the first character:

```
names.OrderBy (s => s.Length)
     .ThenBy (s => s[1]).ThenBy (s => s[0]);
```

The equivalent in comprehension syntax is this:

```
from s in names
orderby s.Length, s[1], s[0]
select s;
```

LINQ also provides OrderByDescending and ThenByDescending operators that do the same things, emitting the results in reverse order. The following LINQ to SQL query retrieves purchases in descending order of price, with those of the same price listed alphabetically:

```
dataContext.Purchases.OrderByDescending (p => p.Price)
                     .ThenBy (p => p.Description);
```

In comprehension syntax:

```
from p in dataContext.Purchases
orderby p.Price descending, p.Description
select p;
```

Comparers and collations

In a local query, the key selector objects themselves determine the ordering algorithm via their default IComparable implementation. You can override the sorting algorithm by passing in an IComparer object. The following performs a case-insensitive sort:

```
names.OrderBy (n => n,
               StringComparer.CurrentCultureIgnoreCase);
```

Passing in a comparer is not supported in comprehension syntax, nor in any way by LINQ to SQL. In LINQ to SQL, the comparison algorithm is determined by the participating column's collation. If the collation is case-sensitive, you can request a case-insensitive sort by calling ToUpper in the key selector:

```
from p in dataContext.Purchases
orderby p.Description.ToUpper( )
select p;
```

IOrderedEnumerable and IOrderedQueryable

The ordering operators return special subtypes of IEnumerable<T>; those in Enumerable return IOrderedEnumerable; and those in Queryable return IOrderedQueryable. These subtypes allow a subsequent ThenBy operator to refine rather than replace the existing ordering.

The additional members that these subtypes define are not publicly exposed, so they present like ordinary sequences.

The fact that they are different types comes into play when building queries progressively:

```
IOrderedEnumerable<string> query1 =
  names.OrderBy (s => s.Length);

IOrderedEnumerable<string> query2 =
  query1.ThenBy (s => s);
```

If we instead declared query1 of type IEnumerable<string>, the second line would not compile—ThenBy requires an input of type IOrderedEnumerable<string>. You can avoid worrying about this by implicitly typing query variables:

```
var query1 = names.OrderBy (s => s.Length);
var query2 = query1.ThenBy (s => s);
```

Implicit typing can create problems of its own, though. The following will not compile:

```
var query = names.OrderBy (s => s.Length);
query = query.Where (n => n.Length > 3);   // Error
```

Based on OrderBy's output sequence type, the compiler infers query to be of type IOrderedEnumerable<string>. However, the Where on the next line returns an ordinary IEnumerable<string> that cannot be assigned back to query. You can work around this either with explicit typing or by calling AsEnumerable( ) after OrderBy:

```
var query = names.OrderBy (s => s.Length).AsEnumerable( );
query = query.Where (n => n.Length > 3);       // OK
```

The equivalent in interpreted queries is to call AsQueryable.

Grouping

Method	Description	SQL equivalents
GroupBy	Groups a sequence into subsequences	GROUP BY

GroupBy

Argument	Type
Input sequence	IEnumerable<TSource>
Key selector	TSource => TKey
Element selector (optional)	TSource => TElement
Comparer (optional)	IEqualityComparer<TKey>

Return type = IEnumerable<IGrouping<TSource,TElement>>

Comprehension syntax

```
group element-expression by key-expression
```

Overview

GroupBy organizes a flat input sequence into sequences of *groups*. For example, the following organizes all the files in *c:\temp* by extension:

```
string[] files = Directory.GetFiles ("c:\\temp");

IEnumerable<IGrouping<string,string>> query =
  files.GroupBy (file => Path.GetExtension (file));
```

or if you're comfortable with implicit typing:

```
var query = files.GroupBy
  (file => Path.GetExtension (file));
```

Here's how to enumerate the result:

```
foreach (IGrouping<string,string> grouping in query)
{
  Console.WriteLine ("Extension: " + grouping.Key);

  foreach (string filename in grouping)
    Console.WriteLine ("   - " + filename);
}

Extension: .pdf
  -- chapter03.pdf
  -- chapter04.pdf
```

```
Extension: .doc
  -- todo.doc
  -- menu.doc
  -- Copy of menu.doc
...
```

Enumerable.GroupBy works by reading the input elements into
a temporary dictionary of lists so that all elements with the
same key end up in the same sublist. It then emits a sequence
of *groupings*. A grouping is a sequence with a Key property:

```
public interface IGrouping <TKey,TElement>
  : IEnumerable<TElement>, IEnumerable
{
  // Key applies to the subsequence as a whole
  TKey Key { get; }
}
```

By default, the elements in each grouping are untransformed
input elements, unless you specify an elementSelector argument. The following projects each input element to uppercase:

```
files.GroupBy (file =>
  Path.GetExtension (file), file => file.ToUpper( ));
```

An elementSelector is independent of the keySelector. In
our case, this means that the Key on each grouping is still in
its original case:

Extension: .pdf
  -- CHAPTER03.PDF
  -- CHAPTER04.PDF
Extension: .doc
  -- TODO.DOC

Note that the subcollections are not emitted in alphabetical
order of key. GroupBy only groups; it does not do any *sorting*—in fact, it preserves the original ordering. To sort, you
must add an OrderBy operator:

```
files
  .GroupBy (file =>
    Path.GetExtension (file), file => file.ToUpper( ))
  .OrderBy (grouping => grouping.Key);
```

GroupBy has a simple and direct translation in comprehension syntax:

```
group element-expr by key-expr
```

Here's our example in comprehension syntax:

```
from file in files
group file.ToUpper( ) by Path.GetExtension (file);
```

As with select, group "ends" a query—unless you add a query continuation clause:

```
from file in files
group file.ToUpper( ) by Path.GetExtension (file)
into grouping
orderby grouping.Key
select grouping;
```

Query continuations are often useful in a group by query. The next query filters out groups that have fewer than five files in them:

```
from file in files
group file.ToUpper( ) by Path.GetExtension (file)
into grouping
where grouping.Count( ) < 5
select grouping;
```

NOTE

A where after a group by is equivalent to HAVING in SQL. It applies to each subsequence or grouping as a whole, rather than the individual elements.

Sometimes you're interested purely in the result of an aggregation on a grouping, and so can abandon the subsequences:

```
string[] votes = { "Bush","Gore","Gore","Bush","Bush" };

IEnumerable<string> query = from vote in votes
                            group vote by vote into g
                            orderby g.Count( ) descending
                            select g.Key;

string winner = query.First( );      // Bush
```

GroupBy in LINQ to SQL

Grouping works in the same way with interpreted queries. If you have association properties set up in LINQ to SQL, you'll find, however, that the need to group arises less frequently than with standard SQL. For instance, to select customers with least two purchases, you don't need to group; the following query does the job nicely:

```
from c in dataContext.Customers
where c.Purchases.Count >= 2
select c.Name + " has made " + c.Purchases.Count
             + " purchases";
```

An example of when you might use grouping is to list total sales by year:

```
from p in dataContext.Purchases
group p.Price by p.Date.Year into salesByYear
select new {
             Year       = salesByYear.Key,
             TotalValue = salesByYear.Sum( )
           };
```

LINQ's grouping operators expose a superset of SQL's "GROUP BY" functionality. Another departure from traditional SQL is there is no obligation to project the variables or expressions used in grouping or sorting.

Grouping by multiple keys

You can group by a composite key using an anonymous type:

```
from n in names
group n by new { FirstLetter = n[0], Length = n.Length };
```

Custom equality comparers

You can pass a custom equality comparer into GroupBy, in a local query, to change the algorithm for key comparison. Rarely is this required, though, because changing the key selector expression is usually sufficient. For instance, the following creates a case-insensitive grouping:

```
group name by name.ToUpper( )
```

Set Operators

Method	Description	SQL equivalents
Concat	Returns a concatenation of elements in each of the two sequences	UNION ALL
Union	Returns a concatenation of elements in each of the two sequences, excluding duplicates	UNION
Intersect	Returns elements present in both sequences	WHERE ... IN ...
Except	Returns elements present in the first, but not the second sequence	EXCEPT or WHERE ... NOT IN ...

Concat and Union

Contact returns all the elements of the first sequence, followed by all the elements of the second. Union does the same, but removes any duplicates:

```
int[] seq1 = { 1, 2, 3 }, seq2 = { 3, 4, 5 };

IEnumerable<int>
  concat = seq1.Concat (seq2),  // { 1, 2, 3, 3, 4, 5 }
  union  = seq1.Union  (seq2);  // { 1, 2, 3, 4, 5 }
```

Intersect and Except

Intersect returns the elements that two sequences have in common. Except returns the elements in the first input sequence that are *not* present in the second:

```
int[] seq1 = { 1, 2, 3 }, seq2 = { 3, 4, 5 };

IEnumerable<int>
  commonality = seq1.Intersect (seq2),    // { 3 }
  difference1 = seq1.Except    (seq2),    // { 1, 2 }
  difference2 = seq2.Except    (seq1);    // { 4, 5 }
```

Enumerable.Except works internally by loading all of the elements in the first collection into a dictionary, then removing from the dictionary all elements present in the second sequence. The equivalent in SQL is a NOT EXISTS or NOT IN subquery:

```
SELECT number FROM numbers1Table
WHERE number NOT IN (SELECT number FROM numbers2Table)
```

Conversion Methods

LINQ deals primarily in sequences; in other words, collections of type IEnumerable<T>. The conversion methods convert to and from, other types of collections:

Method	Description
OfType	Converts IEnumerable to IEnumerable<T>, discarding wrongly typed elements
Cast	Converts IEnumerable to IEnumerable<T>, throwing an exception if there are any wrongly typed elements
ToArray	Converts IEnumerable<T> to T[]
ToList	Converts IEnumerable<T> to List<T>
ToDictionary	Converts IEnumerable<T> to Dictionary<TKey,TValue>
ToLookup	Converts IEnumerable<T> to ILookup<TKey,TElement>
AsEnumerable	Downcasts to IEnumerable<T>
AsQueryable	Casts or converts to IQueryable<T>

OfType and Cast

OfType and Cast accept a nongeneric IEnumerable collection and emit a generic IEnumerable<T> sequence that you can subsequently query:

```
// ArrayList is defined in System.Collections
ArrayList classicList = new ArrayList();
classicList.AddRange ( new int[] { 3, 4, 5 } );
IEnumerable<int> sequence1 = classicList.Cast<int>();
```

Cast and OfType differ in their behavior when encountering an input element that's of an incompatible type. Cast throws an exception; OfType ignores the incompatible element. Continuing the preceding example:

```
DateTime offender = DateTime.Now;
classicList.Add (offender);

IEnumerable<int> sequence2 = classicList
  .OfType<int>( );      // OK - Ignores offending DateTime

IEnumerable<int> sequence3 = classicList
  .Cast<int>( );        // Throws exception
```

The rules for element compatibility exactly follow those of C#'s is operator. We can see this by examining the internal implementation of OfType:

```
public static IEnumerable<TSource> OfType <TSource>
  (IEnumerable source)
{
  foreach (object element in source)
    if (element is TSource)
      yield return (TSource)element;
}
```

Cast has an identical implementation, except that it omits the type compatibility test:

```
public static IEnumerable<TSource> Cast <TSource>
  (IEnumerable source)
{
  foreach (object element in source)
    yield return (TSource)element;
}
```

A consequence of these implementations is that you cannot use Cast to convert elements from one value type to another (for this, you must perform a Select operation instead). In other words, Cast is not as flexible as C#'s cast operator, which also allows static type conversions such as the following:

```
int i = 3;
long l = i;            // Static conversion int->long
int i2 = (int) l;      // Static conversion long->int
```

We can demonstrate this by attempting to use OfType or Cast to convert a sequence of ints to a sequence of longs:

```
int[] integers = { 1, 2, 3 };

IEnumerable<long> test1 = integers.OfType<long>();
IEnumerable<long> test2 = integers.Cast<long>();
```

When enumerated, test1 emits zero elements and test2 throws an exception. Examining OfType's implementation, it's fairly clear why. After substituting TSource, we get the following expression:

```
(element is long)
```

which returns false for an int element, due to the lack of an inheritance relationship.

As we suggested previously, the solution is to use an ordinary Select:

```
IEnumerable<long> castLong =
    integers.Select (s => (long) s);
```

OfType and Cast are also useful in downcasting elements in a generic input sequence. For instance, if you had an input sequence of type IEnumerable<Fruit>, OfType<Apple> would return just the apples. This is particularly useful in LINQ to XML.

ToArray, ToList, ToDictionary, ToLookup

ToArray and ToList emit the results into an array or generic list. These operators force the immediate enumeration of the input sequence (unless indirected via a subquery or expression tree). For examples, refer to the earlier "Deferred Execution" section.

ToDictionary and ToLookup accept the following arguments:

Argument	Type
Input sequence	IEnumerable<TSource>
Key selector	TSource => TKey

Argument	Type
Element selector (optional)	TSource => TElement
Comparer (optional)	IEqualityComparer<TKey>

ToDictionary also forces immediate execution of a sequence, writing the results to a generic Dictionary. The keySelector expression you provide must evaluate to a unique value for each element in the input sequence; otherwise, an exception is thrown. In contrast, ToLookup allows many elements of the same key. We described lookups earlier in the "Joining with lookups" section.

AsEnumerable and AsQueryable

AsEnumerable upcasts a sequence to IEnumerable<T>, forcing the compiler to bind subsequent query operators to methods in Enumerable, instead of Queryable. For an example, see the the earlier "Interpreted Queries" section.

AsQueryable downcasts a sequence to IQueryable<T> if it implements that interface. Otherwise, it instantiates an IQueryable<T> wrapper over the local query.

Element Operators

Method	Description	SQL equivalents
First, FirstOrDefault	Returns the first element in the sequence, optionally satisfying a predicate	SELECT TOP 1 ... ORDER BY ...
Last, LastOrDefault	Returns the last element in the sequence, optionally satisfying a predicate	SELECT TOP 1 ... ORDER BY ... DESC
Single, SingleOrDefault	Equivalent to First/ FirstOrDefault, but throws an exception if there is more than one match	

Method	Description	SQL equivalents
ElementAt, ElementAtOrDefault	Returns the element at the specified position	Exception thrown
DefaultIfEmpty	Returns null or default(TSource) if the sequence has no elements	OUTER JOIN

Methods ending in "OrDefault" return default(TSource) rather than throw an exception if the input sequence is empty, or if no elements match the supplied predicate.

default(TSource) = null for reference type elements, or "blank" (usually zero) for value type elements.

First, Last, Single

Argument	Type
Source sequence	IEnumerable<TSource>
Predicate (optional)	TSource => bool

The following example demonstrates First and Last:

```
int[] numbers  = { 1, 2, 3, 4, 5 };
int first      = numbers.First();                  // 1
int last       = numbers.Last();                   // 5
int firstEven  = numbers.First  (n => n % 2 == 0); // 2
int lastEven   = numbers.Last   (n => n % 2 == 0); // 4
```

The following demonstrates First versus FirstOrDefault:

```
// Throws an exception:
int firstBigError = numbers.First (n => n > 10);

// Evaluates to 0:
int firstBigNumber = numbers.FirstOrDefault(n => n > 10);
```

To avoid an exception, Single requires exactly one matching element; SingleOrDefault requires one *or zero* matching elements:

```
int divisibleBy3 =
  numbers.Single (n => n % 3 == 0);    // 3

int divisibleBy2Error =
  numbers.Single (n => n % 2 == 0);    // Error: 2 matches

int singleError =
  numbers.Single (n => n > 10);        // Error: no matches

int noMatches =
  numbers.SingleOrDefault (n => n > 10);        // 0

int divisibleBy2Error =
  numbers.SingleOrDefault (n => n % 2 == 0);    // Error
```

Single is the "fussiest" in this family of element operators; FirstOrDefault and LastOrDefault are the most tolerant.

In LINQ to SQL, Single is often used to retrieve a row from a table by primary key:

```
Customer cust =
  dataContext.Customers.Single (c => c.ID == 3);
```

ElementAt

Argument	Type
Source sequence	IEnumerable<TSource>
Index of element to return	int

ElementAt picks the *nth* element from the sequence:

```
int[] numbers  = { 1, 2, 3, 4, 5 };
int third      = numbers.ElementAt (2);          // 3
int tenthError = numbers.ElementAt (9);          // Error
int tenth      = numbers.ElementAtOrDefault (9); // 0
```

Enumerable.ElementAt is written such that if the input sequence happens to implement IList<T>, it calls IList<T>'s indexer. Otherwise, it enumerates *n* times, and then returns the next element. ElementAt is not supported in LINQ to SQL.

DefaultIfEmpty

DefaultIfEmpty converts empty sequences to null/default( ). This is used when writing flat outer joins; see the earlier "Outer joins with SelectMany" and "Flat outer joins" sections.

Aggregation Methods

Method	Description	SQL equivalents
Count, LongCount	Returns the number of elements in the input sequence, optionally satisfying a predicate	COUNT( )
Min, Max	Returns the smallest or largest element in the sequence	MIN( ), MAX( )
Sum, Average	Calculates a numeric sum or average over elements in the sequence	SUM( ), AVG ()
Aggregate	Performs a custom aggregation	Exception thrown

Count and LongCount

Argument	Type
Source sequence	IEnumerable<TSource>
Predicate (optional)	TSource => bool

Count simply enumerates over a sequence, returning the number of items:

```
int fullCount = new int[] { 5, 6, 7 }.Count();    // 3
```

The internal implementation of Enumerable.Count tests the input sequence to see whether it happens to implement ICollection<T>. If it does, it simply calls ICollection<T>. Count. Otherwise, it enumerates over every item, incrementing a counter.

You can optionally supply a predicate:

```
int digitCount =
  "pa55w0rd".Count (c => char.IsDigit (c));   // 3
```

LongCount does the same job as Count, but returns a 64-bit integer, allowing for sequences of greater than 2 billion elements.

Min and Max

Argument	Type
Source sequence	IEnumerable<TSource>
Result selector (optional)	TSource => TResult

Min and Max return the smallest or largest element from a sequence:

```
int[] numbers = { 28, 32, 14 };
int smallest = numbers.Min();   // 14;
int largest  = numbers.Max();   // 32;
```

If you include a selector expression, each element is first projected:

```
int smallest = numbers.Max (n => n % 10);   // 8;
```

A selector expression is mandatory if the items themselves are not intrinsically comparable—in other words, if they do not implement IComparable<T>:

```
Purchase runtimeError =
  dataContext.Purchases.Min();       // Runtime error

decimal? lowestPrice =
  dataContext.Purchases.Min (p => p.Price);   // OK
```

A selector expression determines not only how elements are compared, but also the final result. In the preceding example, the final result is a decimal value, not a purchase object. To get the cheapest purchase, you need a subquery:

```
Purchase cheapest = dataContext.Purchases
  .Where (p => p.Price ==
          dataContext.Purchases.Min (p2 => p2.Price))
  .FirstOrDefault( );
```

In this case, you could also formulate the query without an aggregation—using an OrderBy followed by FirstOrDefault.

Sum and Average

Argument	Type
Source sequence	IEnumerable<TSource>
Result selector (optional)	TSource => TResult

Sum and Average are aggregation operators that are used in similar manner to Min and Max:

```
decimal[] numbers  = { 3, 4, 8 };
decimal sumTotal   = numbers.Sum( );       // 15
decimal average    = numbers.Average( );   // 5 (mean)
```

The following returns the total length of each of the strings in the names array:

```
int combinedLength = names.Sum (s => s.Length);   // 19
```

Sum and Average are fairly restrictive in their typing. Their definitions are hard wired to each of the numeric types (int, long, float, double, decimal, and their nullable versions). In contrast, Min and Max can operate directly on anything that implements IComparable<T>—such as a string, for instance.

Further, Average always returns either decimal or double, according to the following table.

Selector type	Result type
decimal	decimal
int, long, float, double	double

This means the following does not compile ("cannot convert double to int"):

```
int avg = new int[] { 3, 4 }.Average();
```

But this will compile:

```
double avg = new int[] { 3, 4 }.Average();    // 3.5
```

Average implicitly upscales the input values to avoid loss of precision. In this example, we averaged integers and got 3.5, without needing to resort to an input element cast:

```
double avg = numbers.Average (n => (double) n);
```

In LINQ to SQL, Sum and Average translate to the standard SQL aggregations. The following query returns customers whose average purchase was more than $500:

```
from c in dataContext.Customers
where c.Purchases.Average (p => p.Price) > 500
select c.Name;
```

Aggregate

Aggregate allows you to plug a custom accumulation algorithm for implementing unusual aggregations. Aggregate is not supported in LINQ to SQL and is somewhat specialized in its use cases. The following demonstrates how Aggregate can do the work of Sum:

```
int[] numbers = { 1, 2, 3 };
int sum = numbers.Aggregate (0, (seed, n) => seed + n);
```

The first argument to Aggregate is the *seed*, from which accumulation starts. The second argument is an expression to update the accumulated value, given a fresh element. You can optionally supply a third argument to project the final result value from the accumulated value.

The difficulty with Aggregate is that a simple scalar type rarely serves the job as a useful accumulator. To calculate an average, for instance, you need to keep a running tally of the number of the elements—as well as the sum. Writing a custom accumulator type solves the problem, but it is

---

uneconomical compared to the conventional approach of using a simple foreach loop to calculate the aggregation.

Quantifiers

Method	Description	SQL equivalents
Contains	Returns true if the input sequence contains the given element	WHERE ... IN (...)
Any	Returns true if any elements satisfy the given predicate	WHERE ... IN (...)
All	Returns true if all elements satisfy the given predicate	WHERE (...)
SequenceEqual	Returns true if the second sequence has identical elements to the input sequence	

Contains and Any

The Contains method accepts an argument of type TSource; Any accepts an optional *predicate*.

Contains returns true if the given element is present:

```
bool isTrue = new int[] { 2, 3, 4 }.Contains (3);
```

Any returns true if the given expression is true for at least one element. We can rewrite the preceding query with Any as follows:

```
bool isTrue = new int[] { 2, 3, 4 }.Any (n => n == 3);
```

Any can do everything that Contains can do, and more:

```
bool isFalse = new int[] { 2, 3, 4 }.Any (n => n > 10);
```

Calling Any without a predicate returns true if the sequence has one or more elements. Here's another way to write the preceding query:

```
bool isFalse = new int[] { 2, 3, 4 }
                   .Where (n => n > 10).Any( );
```

Any is particularly useful in subqueries.

All and SequenceEqual

All returns true if all elements satisfy a predicate. The following returns customers whose purchases are less than $100:

```
dataContext.Customers.Where
  (c => c.Purchases.All (p => p.Price < 100));
```

SequenceEqual compares two sequences. To return true, each sequence must have identical elements, in the identical order.

Generation Methods

Method	Description
Empty	Creates an empty sequence
Repeat	Creates a sequence of repeating elements
Range	Creates a sequence of integers

Empty, Repeat, and Range are static (nonextension) methods that manufacture simple local sequences.

Empty

Empty manufactures an empty sequence and requires just a type argument:

```
foreach (string s in Enumerable.Empty<string>())
  Console.Write (s);              // <nothing>
```

In conjunction with the ?? operator, Empty does the reverse of DefaultIfEmpty. For example, suppose we have a jagged array of integers, and we want to get all the integers into a single flat list. The following SelectMany query fails if any of the inner arrays is null:

```
int[][] numbers =
{
  new int[] { 1, 2, 3 },
  new int[] { 4, 5, 6 },
  null            // this null makes the query below fail.
};
```

```
IEnumerable<int> flat =
  numbers.SelectMany (innerArray => innerArray);
```

Empty in conjunction with ?? fixes the problem:

```
IEnumerable<int> flat = numbers
  .SelectMany (innerArray =>
              innerArray ?? Enumerable.Empty <int>() );

foreach (int i in flat)
  Console.Write (i + " ");      // 1 2 3 4 5 6
```

Range and Repeat

Range and Repeat work only with integers. Range accepts a starting index and count:

```
foreach (int i in Enumerable.Range (5, 5))
  Console.Write (i + " ");               // 5 6 7 8 9
```

Repeat accepts the number to repeat and the number of iterations:

```
foreach (int i in Enumerable.Repeat (5, 3))
  Console.Write (i + " ");               // 5 5 5
```

LINQ to XML

The .NET Framework provides a number of APIs for work-ing with XML data. From Framework 3.5, the primary choice for general-purpose XML document processing is LINQ to XML. LINQ to XML comprises a lightweight LINQ-friendly XML document object model, and a set of supplementary query operators. In most scenarios, it can be considered a complete replacement for the preceding W3C-compliant DOM, a.k.a. XmlDocument.

NOTE

The LINQ to XML DOM is extremely well designed and highly performant. Even without LINQ, the LINQ to XML DOM is valuable as a lightweight facade over the low-level XmlReader and XmlWriter classes.

All LINQ to XML types are defined in the System.Xml.Linq namespace.

Architectural Overview

Consider the following XML file:

```
<?xml version="1.0" encoding="utf-8" standalone="yes"?>
<customer id="123" status="archived">
  <firstname>Joe</firstname>
  <lastname>Bloggs</lastname>
</customer>
```

As with all XML files, we start with a *declaration*, and then a root *element*, whose name is customer. The customer element has two *attributes*, each with a name (id and status) and value ("123" and "archived"). Within customer, there are two child elements, firstname and lastname, each having simple text content ("Joe" and "Bloggs").

Each of these constructs—declaration, element, attribute, value, and text content—can be represented with a class. And if such classes have collection properties for storing child content, we can assemble a *tree* of objects to fully describe a document. This is called a *document object model*, or DOM.

LINQ to XML comprises two things:

* An XML DOM, which we call the X-DOM
* A set of about 10 supplementary query operators

As you might expect, the X-DOM consists of types such as XDocument, XElement, and XAttribute. Interestingly, the X-DOM types are not tied to LINQ—you can load, instantiate, update, and save an X-DOM without ever writing a LINQ query.

Conversely, you could use LINQ to query a DOM created of the older W3C-compliant types. However, this would be frustrating and limiting. The distinguishing feature of the X-DOM is that it's LINQ-friendly, meaning:

- It has methods that emit useful `IEnumerable` sequences, upon which you can query.

- Its constructors are designed such that you can build an X-DOM tree through a LINQ projection.

X-DOM Overview

Figure 11 shows the core X-DOM types. `XElement` is the most frequently used of these. `XObject` is the root of the *inheritance* hierarchy; `XElement` and `XDocument` are roots of the *containership* hierarchy.

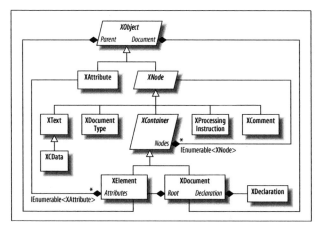

Figure 11. Core X-DOM types

Figure 12 shows the X-DOM tree created from the following code:

```
string xml =
@"<customer id='123' status='archived'>
  <firstname>Joe</firstname>
  <lastname>Bloggs<!--nice name--></lastname>
</customer>";

XElement customer = XElement.Parse (xml);
```

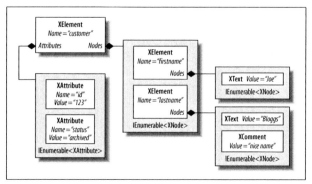

Figure 12. A simple X-DOM tree

XObject is the abstract base class for all XML content. It defines a link to the Parent element in the containership tree as well as an optional XDocument.

XNode is the base class for most XML content, excluding attributes. The distinguishing feature of XNode is that it can sit in an ordered collection of mixed-type XNodes. For instance, consider the following XML:

```
<data>
   Hello world
   <subelement1/>
   <!--comment-->
   <subelement2/>
</data>
```

Within the parent element <data>, there's first an XText node (Hello world), then an XElement node, then an XComment node, and then a second XElement node. In contrast, an XAttribute will tolerate only other XAttributes as peers.

Although an XNode can access its parent XElement, it has no concept of *child* nodes; this is the job of its subclass XContainer. XContainer defines members for dealing with children and is the abstract base class for XElement and XDocument.

XElement introduces members for managing attributes—as well as a Name and Value. In the (fairly common) case of an element having a single XText child node, the Value property on XElement encapsulates this child's content for both get and set operations, cutting unnecessary navigation. Thanks to Value, you can mostly avoid working directly with XText nodes.

XDocument represents the root of an XML tree. More precisely, it *wraps* the root XElement, adding an XDeclaration, processing instructions, and other root-level "fluff." Unlike with the W3C DOM, its use is optional: you can load, manipulate, and save an X-DOM without ever creating an XDocument! The non-reliance on XDocument also means you can efficiently and easily move a node subtree to another X-DOM hierarchy.

Loading and Parsing

Both XElement and XDocument provide static Load and Parse methods to build an X-DOM tree from an existing source:

- Load builds an X-DOM from a file, URI, TextReader, or XmlReader.
- Parse builds an X-DOM from a string.

NOTE

XNode also provides a static ReadFrom method, which instantiates and populates any type of node from an XmlReader. Unlike Load, it stops after reading one (complete) node, so you can continue to read manually from the XmlReader afterward.

You can also do the reverse, and use an XmlReader or XmlWriter to read or write an XNode, via its CreateReader and CreateWriter methods.

For example:

```
XDocument fromWeb = XDocument.Load
  ("http://albahari.com/sample.xml");

XElement fromFile = XElement.Load
  (@"e:\media\somefile.xml");

XElement config = XElement.Parse (
@"<configuration>
    <client enabled='true'>
      <timeout>30</timeout>
    </client>
  </configuration>");
```

Saving and Serializing

Calling ToString on any node converts its content to an XML string—formatted with line breaks and indentation as we just saw. (You can disable the line breaks and indentation by specifying SaveOptions.DisableFormatting when calling ToString.)

XElement and XDocument also provide a Save method that writes an X-DOM to a file, TextWriter, or XmlWriter. If you specify a file, an XML declaration is automatically written. There is also a WriteTo method defined in the XNode class, which accepts just an XmlWriter.

We describe the handling of XML declarations when saving in more detail in the upcoming "Documents and Declarations" section.

Instantiating an X-DOM

Rather than use the Load or Parse methods, you can build an X-DOM tree by manually instantiating objects and adding them to a parent via XContainer's Add method.

To construct an XElement and XAttribute, you simply provide a name and value:

```
XElement lastName = new XElement ("lastname", "Bloggs");
lastName.Add (new XComment ("nice name"));

XElement customer = new XElement ("customer");
customer.Add (new XAttribute ("id", 123));
customer.Add (new XElement ("firstname", "Joe"));
customer.Add (lastName);

Console.WriteLine (customer.ToString());
```

The result:

```
<customer id="123">
  <firstname>Joe</firstname>
  <lastname>Bloggs<!--nice name--></lastname>
</customer>
```

A value is optional when constructing an XElement—you can provide just the element name and add content later. Notice that when we did provide a value, a simple string sufficed— we didn't need to explicitly create and add an XText child node. The X-DOM does this work automatically, so you can deal simply with "values."

Functional Construction

In our preceding example, it's hard to glean the XML structure from the code. X-DOM supports another mode of instantiation called *functional construction* (from functional programming). With functional construction, you build an entire tree in a single expression:

```
XElement customer =
  new XElement ("customer", new XAttribute ("id", 123),
    new XElement ("firstname", "joe"),
    new XElement ("lastname", "bloggs",
      new XComment ("nice name")
    )
  );
```

This has two benefits. First, the code resembles the shape of the XML. Second, it can be incorporated into the select clause of a LINQ query. For example, the following LINQ to SQL query projects directly into an X-DOM:

```
XElement query =
  new XElement ("customers",
    from c in dataContext.Customers
    select
      new XElement ("customer",
        new XAttribute ("id", c.ID),
        new XElement ("firstname", c.FirstName),
        new XElement ("lastname", c.LastName,
          new XComment ("nice name")
        )
      )
  );
```

More on this in the upcoming "Projecting into an X-DOM" section.

Specifying Content

Functional construction is possible because the constructors for XElement (and XDocument) are overloaded to accept a params object array:

```
public XElement (XName name, params object[] content)
```

The same holds true for the Add method in XContainer:

```
public void Add (params object[] content)
```

Hence you can specify any number of child objects of any type when building or appending an X-DOM. This works because *anything* counts as legal content. To see how, we need to examine how each content object is processed internally. Here are the decisions made by XContainer, in order:

1. If the object is null, it's ignored.

2. If the object is based on XNode or XStreamingElement, it's added as is to the Nodes collection.

3. If the object is an XAttribute, it's added to the Attributes collection.

4. If the object is a string, it gets wrapped in an XText node and added to Nodes.

5. If the object implements IEnumerable, it's enumerated and the same rules are applied to each element.

6. Otherwise, the object is converted to a string, wrapped in an XText node, and then added to Nodes.*

Everything ends up in one of two buckets: Nodes or Attributes. Furthermore, any object is valid content because it can always ultimately call ToString on it and treat it as an XText node.

NOTE

Before calling ToString on an arbitrary type, XContainer first tests whether it is one of the following types:

```
float, double, decimal, bool,
DateTime, DateTimeOffset, TimeSpan
```

If so, it calls an appropriate typed ToString method on the XmlConvert helper class instead of calling ToString on the object itself. This ensures that the data is round-trippable and compliant with standard XML-formatting rules.

Automatic Deep Cloning

When a node or attribute is added to an element (whether via functional construction or an Add method), the node or attribute's Parent property is set to that element. A node can have only one parent element: if you add an already parented node to a second parent, the node is automatically *deep-cloned*. This automatic duplication keeps X-DOM object instantiation free of side effects—another hallmark of functional programming.

---

* The X-DOM actually optimizes this step internally by storing simple text content in a string. The XText node is not actually created until you call Nodes( ) on the XContainer.

Navigating/Querying an X-DOM

As you might expect, the XNode and XContainer classes define methods and properties for traversing the X-DOM tree. Unlike a conventional DOM, however, these functions don't return a collection that implements IList<T>. Instead, they return either a single value or a *sequence* that implements IEnumerable<T>—upon which you are then expected to execute a LINQ query (or enumerate with a foreach). This allows for advanced queries as well as simple navigation tasks—using familiar LINQ query syntax.

NOTE

Element and attribute names are case-sensitive in the X-DOM—just as they are in XML.

Child Node Navigation

Return type	Members	Works on
XNode	FirstNode	XContainer
	LastNode	XContainer
IEnumerable<XNode>	Nodes()	XContainer*
	DescendantNodes()	XContainer*
	DescendantNodesAndSelf()	XElement*
XElement	Element (XName)	XContainer
IEnumerable<XElement>	Elements()	XContainer*
	Elements(XName)	XContainer*
	Descendants()	XContainer*
	Descendants(XName)	XContainer*
	DescendantsAndSelf()	XElement*
	DescendantsAndSelf(XName)	XElement*
bool	HasElements	XElement

FirstNode, LastNode, and Nodes

FirstNode and LastNode give you direct access to the first or last child node; Nodes returns all children as a sequence. All three functions consider only direct descendants.

Retrieving elements

The Elements method returns just the child nodes of type XElement. For example:

```
var bench = new XElement ("bench",
             new XElement ("toolbox",
               new XElement ("handtool", "Hammer"),
               new XElement ("handtool", "Rasp")
             ),
             new XElement ("toolbox",
               new XElement ("handtool", "Saw"),
               new XElement ("powertool", "Nailgun")
             ),
             new XComment ("Careful with the nailgun")
           );

foreach (XElement e in bench.Elements())
  Console.WriteLine (e.Name + "=" + e.Value);

// RESULT: toolbox=HammerRasp
           toolbox=SawNailgun
```

The following LINQ query finds the toolbox with the nail gun:

```
IEnumerable<string> query =
  from toolbox in bench.Elements()
  where toolbox.Elements().Any
    (tool => tool.Value == "Nailgun")
  select toolbox.Value;

RESULT: { "SawNailgun" }
```

NOTE

Elements itself is equivalent to a LINQ query on Nodes. Our preceding query could be started as follows:

```
from toolbox in bench.Nodes().OfType<XElement>()
where ...
```

The next example uses a SelectMany query to retrieve the hand tools in all toolboxes:

```
IEnumerable<string> query =
  from toolbox in bench.Elements()
  from tool in toolbox.Elements()
  where tool.Name == "handtool"
  select tool.Value;

RESULT: { "Hammer", "Rasp", "Saw" }
```

Elements can also return just the elements of a given name. For example:

```
int x = bench.Elements ("toolbox").Count();      // 2
```

This is equivalent to:

```
int x = bench.Elements()
             .Where (e => e.Name == "toolbox")
             .Count();                            // 2
```

Elements is also defined as an extension method accepting IEnumerable<XContainer>. More precisely, it accepts an argument of this type:

```
IEnumerable<T> where T : XContainer
```

This allows it to work with sequences of elements too. Using this method, we can rewrite the query that finds the hand tools in all toolboxes as follows:

```
from tool in bench.Elements ("toolbox")
                   .Elements ("handtool")
select tool.Value.ToUpper( );
```

The first call to Elements binds to XContainer's instance method; the second call to it binds to the extension method.

Retrieving a single element

The method Element (singular) returns the first matching element of the given name. Element is useful for simple navigation, as follows:

```
var settings = XElement.Load ("databaseSettings.xml");

string cx = settings.Element ("database")
                   .Element ("connectString")
                   .Value;
```

Element is equivalent to calling Elements( ) and then applying LINQ's FirstOrDefault query operator with a name matching predicate. Element returns null if the requested element doesn't exist.

NOTE

Element("xyz").Value will throw a NullReferenceException if element xyz does not exist. If you'd prefer a null rather than an exception, cast the XElement to a string instead of querying its Value property. In other words:

```
string xyz =
   (string) settings.Element ("xyz");
```

This works because XElement defines an explicit string conversion—just for this purpose!

Recursive functions

XContainer also provides Descendants and DescendantNodes methods, which return child elements or nodes, *recursively*. Descendants accepts an optional element name. Returning to our earlier example, we can use Descendants to find all the hand tools as follows:

```
Console.WriteLine
  (bench.Descendants ("handtool").Count());   // 3
```

Both parent and leaf nodes are included in a *depth-first* traversal. The following query extracts all comments anywhere within the X-DOM that contain the word "careful":

```
IEnumerable<string> query =
  from c in bench.DescendantNodes().OfType<XComment>()
  where c.Value.Contains ("careful")
  orderby c.Value
  select c.Value;
```

Parent Navigation

All XNodes have a Parent property and Ancestor*XXX* methods for parent navigation. A parent is always an XElement:

Return type	Members	Works on
XElement	Parent { get; }	XNode*
Enumerable <XElement>	Ancestors()	XNode*
	Ancestors (XName)	XNode*
	AncestorsAndSelf()	XElement*
	AncestorsAndSelf(XName)	XElement*

If x is an XElement, the following always prints true:

```
foreach (XNode child in x.Nodes())
  Console.WriteLine (child.Parent == x);
```

It is not the same case, however, if x is an XDocument. XDocument is peculiar: it can have children, but can never be anyone's parent! To access the XDocument, you instead use the Document property—this works on any object in the X-DOM tree.

Ancestors returns a sequence whose first element is Parent, and whose next element is Parent.Parent, and so on until the root element.

NOTE

You can navigate to the root element with the LINQ query AncestorsAndSelf().Last().

Another way to achieve the same thing is to call Document.Root—although this works only if an XDocument is present.

Peer Node Navigation

Return type	Members	Defined in
bool	IsBefore (XNode) IsAfter (XNode)	XNode XNode
XNode	PreviousNode NextNode	XNode XNode
IEnumerable <XNode>	NodesBeforeSelf() NodesAfterSelf()	XNode XNode
IEnumerable <XElement>	ElementsBeforeSelf() ElementsBeforeSelf(XName) ElementsAfterSelf() ElementsAfterSelf(XName)	XNode XNode XNode XNode

With PreviousNode and NextNode (and FirstNode/LastNode), you can traverse nodes with the feel of a linked list. This is noncoincidental: internally, nodes are stored in a linked list.

WARNING

XNode internally uses a *singly* linked list, so PreviousNode is nonperformant.

Attribute Navigation

Return type	Members	Defined in
bool	HasAttributes	XElement
XAttribute	Attribute(XName) FirstAttribute LastAttribute	XElement XElement XElement
IEnumerable <XAttribute>	Attributes() Attributes(XName)	XElement XElement

In addition, XAttribute defines PreviousAttribute and NextAttribute properties, as well as Parent.

The Attributes method that accepts a name returns a sequence with either zero or one element; an element cannot have duplicate attribute names in XML.

Updating an X-DOM

You can update elements and attributes in the following ways:

- Call SetValue or reassign the Value property.
- Call SetElementValue or SetAttributeValue.
- Call one of the RemoveXXX methods.
- Call one the of the AddXXX or ReplaceXXX methods, specifying fresh content.

You can also reassign the Name property on XElement objects.

Simple Value Updates

Members	Works on
SetValue (object)	XElement, XAttribute
Value	XElement, XAttribute

The SetValue method replaces an element or attribute's content with a simple value. Setting the Value property does the same, but accepts string data only. We describe both of these functions in detail later (see the upcoming "Working with Values" section).

An effect of calling SetValue (or reassigning Value) is that it replaces all child nodes:

```
XElement settings = new XElement ("settings",
                      new XElement ("timeout", 30)
                    );
settings.SetValue ("blah");
Console.WriteLine (settings.ToString());

// RESULT: <settings>blah</settings>
```

Updating Child Nodes and Attributes

Category	Members	Works on
Add	Add (params object[])	XContainer
	AddFirst (params object[])	XContainer
Remove	RemoveNodes()	XContainer
	RemoveAttributes()	XElement
	RemoveAll()	XElement
Update	ReplaceNodes (params object[])	XContainer
	ReplaceAttributes (params object[])	XElement
	ReplaceAll (params object[])	XElement
	SetElementValue (XName, object)	XElement
	SetAttributeValue (XName, object)	XElement

The most convenient methods in this group are the last two: SetElementValue and SetAttributeValue. They serve as shortcuts for instantiating an XElement or XAttribute and then Adding it to a parent, replacing any existing element or attribute of that name:

```
XElement settings = new XElement ("settings");
settings.SetElementValue ("timeout", 30);  // Adds child
settings.SetElementValue ("timeout", 60);  // Updates it
```

Add appends a child node to an element or document. AddFirst does the same thing, but it inserts at the beginning of the collection rather than at the end.

You can remove all child nodes or attributes in one hit with RemoveNodes or RemoveAttributes. RemoveAll is equivalent to calling both of these methods.

The Replace*XXX* methods are equivalent to Removing and then Adding. They take a snapshot of the input, so e.ReplaceNodes(e.Nodes()) works as expected.

Updating Through the Parent

Members	Works on
AddBeforeSelf (params object[])	XNode
AddAfterSelf (params object[])	XNode
Remove( )	XNode*, XAttribute*
ReplaceWith (params object[])	XNode

The methods AddBeforeSelf, AddAfterSelf, Remove, and ReplaceWith don't operate on the node's children. Instead, they operate on the collection the node itself is in. This requires that the node have a parent element—otherwise, an exception is thrown. AddBeforeSelf and AddAfterSelf are useful for inserting a node into an arbitrary position:

```
XElement items = new XElement ("items",
                    new XElement ("one"),
                    new XElement ("three")
                );
items.FirstNode.AddAfterSelf (new XElement ("two"));
```

Here's the result:

```
<items><one /><two /><three /></items>
```

Inserting into an arbitrary position within a long sequence of elements is actually quite efficient because nodes are stored internally in a linked list.

The Remove method removes the current node from its parent. ReplaceWith does the same and then inserts some other content at the same position. For instance:

```
XElement items = XElement.Parse
  ("<items><one/><two/><three/></items>");
items.FirstNode.ReplaceWith
  (new XComment ("One was here"));
```

Here's the result:

```
<items><!--one was here--><two /><three /></items>
```

Removing a sequence of nodes or attributes

Thanks to extension methods in System.Xml.Linq, you can also call Remove on a *sequence* of nodes or attributes. Consider this X-DOM:

```
XElement contacts = XElement.Parse (
@"<contacts>
    <customer name='Mary'/>
    <customer name='Chris' archived='true'/>
    <supplier name='Susan'>
      <phone archived='true'>
          012345678
          <!--confidential-->
      </phone>
    </supplier>
  </contacts>");
```

The following removes all customers:

```
contacts.Elements ("customer").Remove( );
```

The next statement removes all archived contacts (so "Chris" disappears):

```
contacts.Elements()
  .Where (e => (bool?) e.Attribute ("archived") == true)
  .Remove();
```

NOTE

Internally, the Remove methods first read all matching elements into a temporary list, and then enumerate over the temporary list to perform the deletions. This avoids errors that could otherwise result from deleting and querying at the same time.

If we replaced Elements() with Descendants(), all archived elements throughout the DOM would disappear, with this result:

```
<contacts>
  <customer name="Mary" />
  <supplier name="Susan" />
</contacts>
```

The next example removes all contacts that feature the comment "confidential" anywhere in their tree:

```
contacts.Elements()
  .Where (
         e => e.DescendantNodes()
              .OfType<XComment>()
              .Any (c => c.Value == "confidential")
        ).Remove();
```

This is the result:

```
<contacts>
  <customer name="Mary" />
  <customer name="Chris" archived="true" />
</contacts>
```

Contrast this with the following simpler query, which strips all comment nodes from the tree:

```
contacts.DescendantNodes().OfType<XComment>().Remove();
```

Working with Values

XElement and XAttribute both have a Value property of type string. If an element has a single XText child node, XElement's Value property acts as a convenient shortcut to the content of that node. With XAttribute, the Value property is simply the attribute's value.

Despite the storage differences, the X-DOM provides a consistent set of operations for working with element and attribute values.

Setting Values

There are two ways to assign a value: call SetValue or assign the Value property. SetValue is more flexible because it accepts not just strings, but other simple data types too:

```
var e = new XElement ("date", DateTime.Now);
e.SetValue (DateTime.Now.AddDays(1));
Console.Write (e.Value);

// RESULT: 2007-12-19T16:39:10.734375+09:00
```

We could have instead just set the element's Value property, but this would mean manually converting the DateTime to a string. This is more complicated than calling ToString—it requires the use of XmlConvert for an XML-compliant result.

When you pass a *value* into XElement or XAttribute's constructor, the same automatic conversion takes place for non-string types. This ensures that DateTimes is correctly formatted; true is written in lowercase, and double. NegativeInfinity is written as "-INF."

Getting Values

To go the other way around and parse a Value back to a base type, you simply cast the XElement or XAttribute to the desired type. It sounds like it shouldn't work—but it does! For instance:

```
XElement e = new XElement ("now", DateTime.Now);
DateTime dt = (DateTime) e;

XAttribute a = new XAttribute ("resolution", 1.234);
double res = (double) a;
```

An element or attribute doesn't store DateTimes or numbers natively—they're always stored as text, and then parsed as needed. It also doesn't "remember" the original type, so you must cast it correctly to avoid a runtime error. To make your code robust, you can put the cast in a try/catch block, catching a FormatException.

Explicit casts on XElement and XAttribute can parse to the following types:

- All standard numeric types
- string, bool, DateTime, DateTimeOffset, TimeSpan, and Guid
- Nullable<> versions of the aforementioned value types

Casting to a nullable type is useful in conjunction with the Element and Attribute methods because if the requested name doesn't exist, the cast still works. For instance, if x has no timeout element, the first line generates a runtime error and the second line does not:

```
int timeout = (int) x.Element ("timeout");    // Error
int? timeout = (int?) x.Element ("timeout");  // OK
```

You can factor away the nullable type in the final result with the ?? operator. The following evaluates to 1.0 if the resolution attribute doesn't exist:

```
double resolution =
  (double?) x.Attribute ("resolution") ?? 1.0;
```

Casting to a nullable type won't get you out of trouble, though, if the element or attribute *exists* and has an empty (or improperly formatted) value. For this, you must catch a FormatException.

You can also use casts in LINQ queries. The following returns "John":

```
var data = XElement.Parse (
  @"<data>
      <customer id='1' name='Mary' credit='100' />
      <customer id='2' name='John' credit='150' />
      <customer id='3' name='Anne' />
    </data>");

IEnumerable<string> query =
  from cust in data.Elements()
  where (int?) cust.Attribute ("credit") > 100
  select cust.Attribute ("name").Value;
```

Casting to a nullable int avoids a NullReferenceException in
the case of Anne, who has no credit attribute. Another solution would be to add a predicate to the where clause:

```
where cust.Attributes ("credit").Any()
&& (int) cust.Attribute...
```

The same principles apply when querying element values.

Values and Mixed Content Nodes

Given the value of Value, you might wonder when you'd ever
need to deal directly with XText nodes. The answer: when
you have mixed content. For example:

```
<summary>
  An XAttribute is <bold>not</bold> an XNode
</summary>
```

A simple Value property is not enough to capture summary's
content. The summary element contains three children: an
XText node, followed by an XElement, followed by another
XText node. Here's how to construct it:

```
XElement summary = new XElement ("summary",
                    new XText ("An XAttribute is "),
                    new XElement ("bold", "not"),
                    new XText (" an XNode")
                  );
```

Interestingly, we can still query summary's Value—without
getting an exception. Instead, we get a concatenation of each
child's value:

```
An XAttribute is not an XNode
```

It's also legal to reassign summary's Value, at the cost of replacing all previous children with a single new XText node.

Automatic XText Concatenation

When you add simple content to an XElement, the X-DOM appends to the existing XText child rather than creating a new one. In the following examples, e1 and e2 end up with just one child XText element whose value is HelloWorld:

```
var e1 = new XElement ("test", "Hello");
e1.Add ("World");

var e2 = new XElement ("test", "Hello", "World");
```

If you specifically create XText nodes, however, you end up with multiple children:

```
var e = new XElement ("test",
                      new XText ("Hello"),
                      new XText ("World"));
Console.WriteLine (e.Value);           // HelloWorld
Console.WriteLine (e.Nodes().Count()); // 2
```

XElement doesn't concatenate the two XText nodes so the nodes' object identities are preserved.

Documents and Declarations

XDocument

An XDocument wraps a root XElement and allows you to add an XDeclaration, processing instructions, a document type, and root-level comments. An XDocument is optional and can be ignored or omitted: unlike with the W3C DOM, it does not serve as glue to keep everything together.

An XDocument provides the same functional constructors as XElement. And as it's based on XContainer, it also supports the AddXXX, RemoveXXX, and ReplaceXXX methods. Unlike XElement, however, an XDocument can accept only limited content:

- A single XElement object (the "root")
- A single XDeclaration object
- A single XDocumentType object (to reference a DTD)
- Any number of XProcessingInstruction objects
- Any number of XComment objects

NOTE

Of these, only the root XElement is mandatory to have a valid XDocument. The XDeclaration is optional—if omitted, default settings are applied during serialization.

The simplest valid XDocument has just a root element:

```
var doc = new XDocument (
            new XElement ("test", "data")
          );
```

Notice that we didn't include an XDeclaration object. The file generated by calling doc.Save would still contain an XML declaration, however, because one is generated by default.

The next example produces a simple but correct XHTML file, illustrating all the constructs that an XDocument can accept:

```
var styleInstruction = new XProcessingInstruction (
  "xml-stylesheet", "href='styles.css' type='text/css'");

var docType = new XDocumentType ("html",
  "-//W3C//DTD XHTML 1.0 Strict//EN",
  "http://www.w3.org/TR/xhtml1/DTD/xhtml1-strict.dtd",
  null);

XNamespace ns = "http://www.w3.org/1999/xhtml";
var root =
  new XElement (ns + "html",
    new XElement (ns + "head",
      new XElement (ns + "title", "An XHTML page")),
    new XElement (ns + "body",
      new XElement (ns + "p", "This is the content"))
  );
```

```
var doc =
  new XDocument (
    new XDeclaration ("1.0", "utf-8", "no"),
    new XComment ("Reference a stylesheet"),
    styleInstruction,
    docType,
    root);

doc.Save ("test.html");
```

The resultant *test.html* reads as follows:

```
<?xml version="1.0" encoding="utf-8" standalone="no"?>
<!--Reference a stylesheet-->
<?xml-stylesheet href='styles.css' type='text/css'?>
<!DOCTYPE html PUBLIC "-//W3C//DTD XHTML 1.0 Strict//EN"
  "http://www.w3.org/TR/xhtml1/DTD/xhtml1-strict.dtd">
<html xmlns="http://www.w3.org/1999/xhtml">
  <head>
    <title>An XHTML page</title>
  </head>
  <body>
    <p>This is the content</p>
  </body>
</html>
```

XDocument has a Root property that serves as a shortcut for accessing a document's single XElement. The reverse link is provided by XObject's Document property, which works for all objects in the tree:

```
Console.WriteLine (doc.Root.Name.LocalName);    // html
XElement bodyNode = doc.Root.Element (ns + "body");
Console.WriteLine (bodyNode.Document == doc);   // True
```

NOTE

An XDeclaration is not an XNode and does not appear in the document's Nodes collection—unlike comments, processing instructions, and the root element. Instead, it gets assigned to a dedicated property called Declaration. This is why "True" is repeated four and not five times in the last example.

Recall that a document's children have no Parent:

```
Console.WriteLine (doc.Root.Parent == null);    // True
foreach (XNode node in doc.Nodes())
  Console.Write
    (node.Parent == null);                      // TrueTrueTrueTrue
```

XML Declarations

A standard XML file starts with a declaration such as the following:

```
<?xml version="1.0" encoding="utf-8" standalone="yes"?>
```

An XML declaration ensures that the file will be correctly parsed and understood by a reader. XElement and XDocument follow these rules in emitting XML declarations:

- Calling Save with a filename always writes a declaration.
- Calling Save with an XmlWriter writes a declaration unless the XmlWriter is instructed otherwise.
- The ToString method never emits an XML declaration.

NOTE

You can instruct an XmlWriter not to produce a declaration by setting the OmitXmlDeclaration and ConformanceLevel properties of an XmlWriterSettings object when constructing the XmlWriter.

The presence or absence of an XDeclaration object has no effect on whether an XML declaration gets written. The purpose of an XDeclaration is instead to *hint the XML serialization process*—in two ways:

- What text encoding to use
- What to put in the XML declaration's *encoding* and *standalone* attributes (should a declaration be written)

XDeclaration's constructor accepts three arguments, which correspond to the *version*, *encoding*, and *standalone* attributes. In the following example, *test.xml* is encoded in UTF-16:

```
var doc = new XDocument (
            new XDeclaration ("1.0", "utf-16", "yes"),
            new XElement ("test", "data")
         );
doc.Save ("test.xml");
```

NOTE

Whatever you specify for the XML version is ignored by the XML writer: it always writes "1.0".

The encoding must use an IETF code such as "utf-16"—just as it would appear in the XML declaration.

Names and Namespaces

Just as .NET types can have namespaces, so too can XML elements and attributes.

XML namespaces achieve two things. First, rather like namespaces in C#, they help avoid naming collisions. This can become an issue when you merge data from one XML file into another. Second, namespaces assign *absolute* meaning to a name. The name "nil," for instance, could mean anything. Within the *http://www.w3.org/2001/XMLSchema-instance* namespace, however, "nil" means something equivalent to null in C# and comes with specific rules on how it can be applied.

A namespace in XML is defined with the xmlns attribute:

```
<customer xmlns="OReilly.Nutshell.CSharp"/>
```

xmlns is a special reserved attribute. When used in this manner, it performs two functions:

- It specifies a namespace for the element in question.
- It specifies a default namespace for all descendant elements.

You can also specify a namespace with a *prefix*—an alias that you assign to a namespace to avoid repetition. There are two steps—*defining* the prefix and *using* the prefix. You can do both together as follows:

```
<nut:customer xmlns:nut="OReilly.Nutshell.CSharp"/>
```

Two distinct things are happening here. On the right, `xmlns:nut="..."` defines a prefix called `nut` and makes it available to this element and all its descendants. On the left, `nut:customer` assigns the newly allocated prefix to the `customer` element.

A prefixed element *does not* define a default namespace for descendants. In the following XML, `firstname` has an empty namespace:

```
<nut:customer nut:xmlns="OReilly.Nutshell.CSharp">
  <firstname>Joe</firstname>
</customer>
```

To give `firstname` the `OReilly.Nutshell.CSharp` prefix, we must do this:

```
<nut:customer xmlns:nut="OReilly.Nutshell.CSharp">
  <nut:firstname>Joe</firstname>
</customer>
```

XML lets you define prefixes purely for the convenience of your descendants, without assigning any of them to the parent element itself. The following defines two prefixes, `i` and `z`, while leaving the `customer` element itself with an empty namespace:

```
<customer
  xmlns:i="http://www.w3.org/2001/XMLSchema-instance"
  xmlns:z="http://schemas.microsoft.com/Serialization/">
  ...
</customer>
```

(Both namespaces in this example are URIs. It is standard practice to use URIs [that you own]; it ensures namespace uniqueness.)

You can also assign namespaces to attributes; the main difference is that it always requires a prefix. For instance:

```
<customer
  xmlns:nut="OReilly.Nutshell.CSharp" nut:id="123" />
```

Another difference is that an unqualified attribute always has an empty namespace: it never inherits a default namespace from a parent element.

Specifying Namespaces in the X-DOM

So far in this book, we've used just simple strings for XElement and XAttribute names. A simple string corresponds to an XML name with an empty namespace—rather like a .NET type defined in the global namespace.

There are a couple of ways to specify an XML namespace. The first is to enclose it in braces before the local name. For example:

```
var e = new XElement
  ("{http://domain.com/xmlspace}customer", "Bloggs");
Console.WriteLine (e.ToString( ));
```

Here's the resultant XML:

```
<customer xmlns="http://domain.com/xmlspace">
  Bloggs
</customer>
```

The second (and more performant) approach is to use the XNamespace and XName types. Here are their definitions:

```
public sealed class XNamespace
{
  public string NamespaceName { get; }
}
```

```
public sealed class XName
{
  public string LocalName { get; }
  public XNamespace Namespace { get; }   // Optional
}
```

Both types define implicit casts from string, so the following is legal:

```
XNamespace ns    = "http://domain.com/xmlspace";
XName localName  = "customer";
XName fullName   = "{http://domain.com/xmlspace}customer";
```

XName also overloads the + operator, allowing you to combine a namespace and name without using braces:

```
XNamespace ns = "http://domain.com/xmlspace";
XName fullName = ns + "customer";
Console.WriteLine (fullName);

// RESULT: {http://domain.com/xmlspace}customer
```

All constructors and methods in the X-DOM that accept an element or attribute name actually accept an XName object rather than a string. The reason you can substitute a string—as in all our examples to date—is because of the implicit cast.

Specifying a namespace is the same whether for an element or an attribute:

```
XNamespace ns = "http://domain.com/xmlspace";
var data = new XElement (ns + "data",
            new XAttribute (ns + "id", 123)
           );
```

The X-DOM and Default Namespaces

The X-DOM ignores the concept of default namespaces until it comes time to actually output XML. This means that when you construct a child XElement, you must explicitly give it a namespace if needed: it *will not* inherit from the parent:

```
XNamespace ns = "http://domain.com/xmlspace";
var data = new XElement (ns + "data",
            new XElement (ns + "customer", "Bloggs"),
            new XElement (ns + "purchase", "Bicycle")
          );
```

The X-DOM does, however, apply default namespaces when
reading and outputting XML:

```
Console.WriteLine (data.ToString());
```

```
OUTPUT:
  <data xmlns="http://domain.com/xmlspace">
    <customer>Bloggs</customer>
    <purchase>Bicycle</purchase>
  </data>
```

```
Console.WriteLine
  (data.Element (ns + "customer").ToString());
```

```
OUTPUT:
  <customer xmlns="http://domain.com/xmlspace">Bloggs
  </customer>
```

If you construct XElement children without specifying
namespaces—in other words:

```
XNamespace ns = "http://domain.com/xmlspace";
var data = new XElement (ns + "data",
            new XElement ("customer", "Bloggs"),
            new XElement ("purchase", "Bicycle")
          );
Console.WriteLine (data.ToString());
```

you get this result instead:

```
<data xmlns="http://domain.com/xmlspace">
  <customer xmlns="">Bloggs</customer>
  <purchase xmlns="">Bicycle</purchase>
</data>
```

Another trap is failing to include a namespace when navigating an X-DOM:

```
XNamespace ns = "http://domain.com/xmlspace";
var data = new XElement (ns + "data",
            new XElement (ns + "customer", "Bloggs"),
            new XElement (ns + "purchase", "Bicycle")
          );
```

```
XElement x = data.Element (ns + "customer");    // ok
XElement y = data.Element ("customer");          // null
```

If you build an X-DOM tree without specifying namespaces, you can subsequently assign every element to a single namespace as follows:

```
foreach (XElement e in data.DescendantsAndSelf( ))
  if (e.Name.Namespace == "")
    e.Name = ns + e.Name.LocalName;
```

Prefixes

The X-DOM treats prefixes just as it treats namespaces: purely as a serialization function. This means you can choose to completely ignore the issue of prefixes—and get by! The only reason you might want to do otherwise is for efficiency when outputting to an XML file. For example, consider this:

```
XNamespace ns1 = "http://test.com/space1";
XNamespace ns2 = "http://test.com/space2";

var mix = new XElement (ns1 + "data",
            new XElement (ns2 + "element", "value"),
            new XElement (ns2 + "element", "value"),
            new XElement (ns2 + "element", "value")
          );
```

By default, XElement will serialize this as follows:

```
<data xmlns="http://test.com/space1">
  <element xmlns="http://test.com/space2">value</element>
  <element xmlns="http://test.com/space2">value</element>
  <element xmlns="http://test.com/space2">value</element>
</data>
```

As you can see, there's a bit of unnecessary duplication. The solution is *not* to change the way you construct the X-DOM, but to hint the serializer prior to writing the XML. You do this by adding attributes defining prefixes that you want to see applied. This is typically done on the root element:

```
mix.SetAttributeValue (XNamespace.Xmlns + "ns1", ns1);
mix.SetAttributeValue (XNamespace.Xmlns + "ns2", ns2);
```

This assigns the prefix "ns1" to our `XNamespace` variable ns1, and "ns2" to ns2. The X-DOM automatically picks up these attributes when serializing and uses them to condense the resulting XML. Here's the result now of calling `ToString` on mix:

```
<ns1:data xmlns:ns1="http://test.com/space1"
          xmlns:ns2="http://test.com/space2">
  <ns2:element>value</ns2:element>
  <ns2:element>value</ns2:element>
  <ns2:element>value</ns2:element>
</ns1:data>
```

Prefixes don't change the way you construct, query, or update the X-DOM—for these activities you ignore the presence of prefixes and continue to use full names. Prefixes come into play only when converting to and from XML files or streams.

Prefixes are also honored in serializing attributes. In the following example, we record a customer's date of birth and credit as "nil" using the W3C-standard attribute. The highlighted line ensures that the prefix is serialized without unnecessary namespace repetition:

```
XNamespace xsi =
  "http://www.w3.org/2001/XMLSchema-instance";

var nil = new XAttribute (xsi + "nil", true);

var cust =
  new XElement ("customers",
    new XAttribute (XNamespace.Xmlns + "xsi", xsi),
    new XElement ("customer",
      new XElement ("lastname", "Bloggs"),
      new XElement ("dob", nil),
      new XElement ("credit", nil)
    )
  );
```

This is its XML:

```
<customers
  xmlns:xsi="http://www.w3.org/2001/XMLSchema-instance">
  <customer>
    <lastname>Bloggs</lastname>
    <dob xsi:nil="true" />
    <credit xsi:nil="true" />
  </customer>
</customers>
```

For brevity, we predeclared the nil XAttribute so that we could use it twice in building the DOM. You're allowed to reference the same attribute twice because it's automatically duplicated as required.

Projecting into an X-DOM

You can also use LINQ queries to project *into* an X-DOM. The source can be anything over which LINQ can query, such as:

- LINQ to SQL Tables
- A local collection
- Another X-DOM

Regardless of the source, the strategy is the same in using LINQ to emit an X-DOM: you first write a functional construction expression that produces the desired X-DOM shape, and then build a LINQ query around the expression.

For instance, suppose we wanted to retrieve customers from a database into the following XML:

```
<customers>
  <customer id="1">
    <name>Sue</name>
    <buys>3</buys>
  </customer>
  ...
</customers>
```

We start by writing a functional construction expression for the X-DOM using simple literals:

```
var customers =
  new XElement ("customers",
    new XElement ("customer", new XAttribute ("id", 1),
      new XElement ("name", "Sue"),
      new XElement ("buys", 3)
    )
  );
```

We then turn this into a projection and build a LINQ query around it:

```
var customers =
  new XElement ("customers",
    from c in dataContext.Customers
    select
      new XElement ("customer",
        new XAttribute ("id", c.ID),
        new XElement ("name", c.Name),
        new XElement ("buys", c.Purchases.Count)
      )
  );
```

Here's the result:

```
<customers>
  <customer id="1">
    <name>Tom</firstname>
    <buys>3</buys>
  </customer>
  <customer id="2">
    <name>Harry</firstname>
    <buys>2</buys>
  </customer>
    ...
</customers>
```

The outer query in this case defines the line at which the query transitions from being a remote LINQ to SQL query to a local LINQ to enumerable query. XElement's constructor doesn't know about IQueryable<>, so it forces enumeration of the LINQ to SQL query—and execution of the SQL statement.

Eliminating Empty Elements

Suppose in the preceding example that we also wanted to include details of the customer's most recent high-value purchase. We could do this as follows:

```
var customers =
  new XElement ("customers",
    from c in dataContext.Customers
    let lastBigBuy = (from p in c.Purchases
                      where p.Price > 1000
                      orderby p.Date descending
                      select p).FirstOrDefault( )
    select
      new XElement ("customer",
        new XAttribute ("id", c.ID),
        new XElement ("name", c.Name),
        new XElement ("buys", c.Purchases.Count),
        new XElement ("lastBigBuy",
          new XElement ("description",
            lastBigBuy == null
              ? null : lastBigBuy.Description),
          new XElement ("price",
            lastBigBuy == null
              ? 0m : lastBigBuy.Price)
        )
      )
  );
```

This emits empty elements, though, for customers with no high-value purchases. (If it were a local query, not a LINQ to SQL query, a NullReferenceException would be thrown. In such cases, it would be better to omit the lastBigBuy node entirely. We can achieve this by wrapping the constructor for the lastBigBuy element in a conditional operator:

```
select
  new XElement ("customer",
    new XAttribute ("id", c.ID),
    new XElement ("name", c.Name),
    new XElement ("buys", c.Purchases.Count),
    lastBigBuy == null ? null :
      new XElement ("lastBigBuy",
        new XElement ("description",
          lastBigBuy.Description),
        new XElement ("price", lastBigBuy.Price)
```

For customers with no lastBigBuy, a null is emitted instead of an empty XElement. This is what we want because null content is simply ignored.

Streaming a Projection

If you're projecting into an X-DOM only to Save it (or call ToString on it) you can improve memory efficiency through an XStreamingElement. An XStreamingElement is a cut-down version of XElement that applies *deferred loading* semantics to its child content. To use it, you simply replace the outer XElements with XStreamingElements:

```
var customers =
  new XStreamingElement ("customers",
    from c in dataContext.Customers
    select
      new XStreamingElement ("customer",
        new XAttribute ("id", c.ID),
        new XElement ("name", c.Name),
        new XElement ("buys", c.Purchases.Count)
      )
  );
customers.Save ("data.xml");
```

The queries passed into an XStreamingElement's constructor are not enumerated until you call Save, ToString, or WriteTo on the element; this avoids loading the whole X-DOM into memory at once. The flipside is that the queries are reevaluated should you re-Save. Also, you cannot traverse an XStreamingElement's child content—it does not expose methods such as Elements or Attributes.

XStreamingElement is not based on XObject—nor any other class—because it has such a limited set of members. The only members it has, besides Save, ToString, and WriteTo, are the following:

- An Add method, which accepts content like the constructor
- A Name property

XStreamingElement does not allow you to *read* content in a streamed fashion—for this, you must use an XmlReader in conjunction with the X-DOM.

Transforming an X-DOM

You can transform an X-DOM by reprojecting it. For instance, suppose we want to transform an *msbuild* XML file, used by the C# compiler and Visual Studio to describe a project, into a simple format suitable for generating a report. An *msbuild* file looks like this:

```
<Project DefaultTargets="Build"
  xmlns="http://schemas.microsoft.com/dev...>
  <PropertyGroup>
    <Platform Condition=" '$(Platform)' == '' ">
      AnyCPU
    </Platform>
    <ProductVersion>9.0.11209</ProductVersion>
    ...
  </PropertyGroup>
  <ItemGroup>
    <Compile Include="ObjectGraph.cs" />
    <Compile Include="Program.cs" />
    <Compile Include="Properties\AssemblyInfo.cs" />
    <Compile Include="Tests\Aggregation.cs" />
    <Compile Include="Tests\Advanced\RecursiveXml.cs" />
  </ItemGroup>
  <ItemGroup>
    ...
  </ItemGroup>
  ...
</Project>
```

Let's say we wanted to include only files, as follows:

```
<ProjectReport>
  <File>ObjectGraph.cs</File>
  <File>Program.cs</File>
  <File>Properties\AssemblyInfo.cs</File>
  <File>Tests\Aggregation.cs</File>
  <File>Tests\Advanced\RecursiveXml.cs</File>
</ProjectReport>
```

The following query performs this transformation:

```
XElement project = XElement.Load("myProjectFile.csproj");
XNamespace ns = project.Name.Namespace;
var query =
  new XElement ("ProjectReport",
    from compileItem in
      project.Elements (ns + "ItemGroup")
             .Elements (ns + "Compile")
    let include = compileItem.Attribute ("Include")
    where include != null
    select new XElement ("File", include.Value)
  );
```

The query first extracts all ItemGroup elements, and then uses the Elements extension method to obtain a flat sequence of all their Compile subelements. Notice that we had to specify an XML namespace—everything in the original file inherits the namespace defined by the Project element—so a local element name such as ItemGroup won't work on its own. Then, we extracted the Include attribute value and projected its value as an element.

Index

A

Add method, 128, 129
AddAfterSelf method, 130
AddBeforeSelf method, 130
AddFirst method, 129
Aggregate method, 107, 110
aggregation methods, 10,
        107–111
    Aggregate, 107, 110
    Average, 107, 109
    Count, 107
    LongCount, 107
    Max, 107, 108
    Min, 107, 108
    Sum, 107, 109
All method, 111
Ancestors method, 126
AncestorsAndSelf method, 126
anonymous types, 30
Any method, 111
AsEnumerable method, 38–40,
        101, 104
    advantage of using, 40
AsQueryable method, 33, 54,
        95, 101, 104
associations (LINQ to
        SQL), 45–47
Attributes method, 128
Average method, 107, 109

B

building query
        expressions, 52–59
    AsQueryable method, 54
    delegates versus expression
        trees, 53–55
    expression trees, 55–59
        methods, 56

C

callbacks, 7
captured variables, 17
Cast method, 101–103
casting to nullable type, 134
chaining query operators, 4–6
Column attribute, 40
compiling expression trees, 53
composition strategies, 25–28
comprehension queries, 10–14
    from clause, 11
    group clause, 11
    iteration variable, 11, 12
    mixed syntax queries, 14
    OrderBy method, 12
    select clause, 11
    Select method, 12
    using System.Linq
        directive, 12
    Where method, 12

We'd like to hear your suggestions for improving our indexes. Send email to
index@oreilly.com.

Concat method, 10, 100
Contains method, 111
continuations (query), 27
conversion methods, 15,
    101–104
  AsEnumerable, 101, 104
  AsQueryable, 101, 104
  Cast, 101–103
  OfType, 101–103
  ToArray, 101, 103
  ToDictionary, 101, 103
  ToList, 101, 103
  ToLookup, 101, 103
correlated subqueries, 24, 69
Count method, 107
cross join, 77
  LINQ to SQL, 78
cross product, 77
custom equality comparers, 99

D

database schema, 37
DataContext class, 42–44
  multitier applications, 44
  ObjectTrackingEnabled, 43
  SubmitChanges method, 50
DataLoadOptions class, 48–49
  AssociateWith method, 49
  eager loading, 49
decorator sequences, 17
DefaultIfEmpty method, 105,
    107
deferred execution, 15–21, 36
  with LINQ to SQL, 46
deferred loading with XML
    (streaming), 150
delegates versus expression
    trees, 53–55
Descendants method, 122

DescendantsAndSelf
    method, 122
Distinct method, 62, 66
document object model
    (DOM), 114

E

eager loading (LINQ to
    SQL), 49
Element method, 122
element operators, 104–107
  DefaultIfEmpty method, 105,
    107
  ElementAt method, 105, 106
  ElementAtOrDefault
    method, 105
  First method, 104, 105
  FirstOrDefault method, 104,
    105
  Last method, 104, 105
  LastOrDefault method, 104
  Single method, 104, 105
  SingleOrDefault method, 104,
    105
element typing, 8
ElementAt method, 9, 105, 106
ElementAtOrDefault
    method, 105
elements, 1
  mapping input to output, 9
  projected, 5
Elements method, 122
ElementsAfterSelf method, 127
ElementsBeforeSelf method, 127
elementSelector, 97
Empty method, 112
entities (LINQ to SQL), 41
  associations, 45–47
  automatic entity
    generation, 45

EntityRef type, 47
EntitySet, 46
Enumerable class, 2, 4
    AsEnumerable
        method, 38–40
        advantage of using, 40
    query operators, 33
Enumerable.Where, 7
equi-join, 79
Except method, 100
expanding and flattening
        subsequences, 76
Expression class, 56
expression trees, 33, 36, 55–59
    compiling, 53
    methods, 56
    versus delegates, 53–55

F

filtering, 62–66
    Distinct method, 62, 66
    indexed, 64
    Skip method, 62, 65
    SkipWhile method, 62, 66
    Take method, 62, 65
    TakeWhile method, 62, 66
    Where method, 62–65
First method, 9, 104, 105
FirstAttribute method, 128
FirstNode, 123
FirstOrDefault method, 104,
        105, 125
foreign keys, 50
from clause, 11, 67
    multiple from clauses, 73
Func signatures, 7
functional construction (LINQ
        to XML), 119–120

G

generation methods, 112–113
    Empty, 112
    Range, 113
    Repeat, 113
group clause, 97
GroupBy method, 95–99
    custom equality
        comparers, 99
    grouping by multiple keys, 99
    LINQ to SQL, 99
    overview, 96–98
GroupJoin method, 82, 88–91
    flat outer joins, 89
    joining with lookups, 90–91

H

HasAttributes method, 128
HasElements method, 122

I

IEnumerable interface, 1
implicit typing, 3, 30
indexed filtering, 64
interpreted queries, 33–40
    Enumerable.AsEnumerable, 3
        8–40
        advantage of using, 40
    execution, 36–38
    how they work, 35–38
    IQueryable, 33
Intersect method, 100
into keyword, 27
IOrderedEnumerable, 94
IOrderedQueryable, 94
IQueryable, 2, 33
    implementations, 33
IsAfter method, 127
IsBefore method, 127

IsPrimaryKey property, 41
iteration variable, 11, 12
iterators, 18

J

Join method, 82–87
  joining with lookups, 90–91
  lambda syntax, 87
  multiple keys, 86
joining, 82–92
  cross join
    LINQ to SQL, 78
  equi-join, 79
  GroupJoin method, 82, 88–91
    flat outer joins, 89
    joining with
      lookups, 90–91
  Join method, 82–87
    joining with
      lookups, 90–91
    lambda syntax, 87
    multiple keys, 86
  LINQ to SQL, 69–71
  multiple keys, 86
  outer joins
    SelectMany method, 80–82
  SelectMany method, 77
  with lookups, 90–91

L

lambda expressions, 3
  composing, 6–9
  element typing, 8
  Func signatures, 7
lambda queries, 4–10
  chaining query operators, 4–6
  composing lambda
    expressions, 6–9
  natural ordering, 9
  syntax
    joining in, 87
    versus query syntax, 13

LambdaExpression class, 56
Last method, 9, 104, 105
LastAttribute method, 128
LastNode, 123
LastOrDefault method, 104
lazy evaluation, 15
let keyword, 32
LINQ to SQL, 33, 40–52
  associations, 45–47
  automatic entity
    generation, 45
  cross join, 78
  DataContext class, 42–44
    multitier applications, 44
    ObjectTrackingEnabled, 43
  DataLoadOptions
    class, 48–49
    AssociateWith method, 49
    eager loading, 49
  deferred execution, 47–48
  ElementAt method, 106
  entity classes, 40–42
  foreign keys, 50
  GroupBy method, 99
  interpreted queries (see
    interpreted queries)
  SelectMany method, 78–80
  SQL Server, 38
  subqueries and joins, 69–71
  updates, 50–52
  Where method, 64
LINQ to XML, 113–115
  architectural overview, 114
  automatic deep cloning, 121
  containership hierarchy, 115
  default namespaces, 143–145
  documents and
    declarations, 136–140
  functional
    construction, 119–120
    expression, 147
  inheritance hierarchy, 115
  instantiating, 118–121
  loading and parsing, 117

namespaces
  attributes, 143
  elements, 143
navigating and
    querying, 122–128
  attribute navigation, 128
  child node
      navigation, 122–126
  parent navigation, 126
  peer node navigation, 127
overview, 115–118
prefixes, 145–147
projecting into, 147–152
  eliminating empty
      elements, 149
  streaming projection, 150
recursive functions, 126
retrieving elements, 123–125
retrieving single element, 125
saving and serializing, 118
specifying content, 120–121
specifying
    namespaces, 142–143
transforming, 151–152
updating, 128–132
  child nodes and
      attributes, 130
  removing sequence of nodes
      or attributes, 131
  simple value updates, 129
  through parent, 130–132
working with values, 133–136
Load method, 117
local queries, 33
local sequence, 2
LongCount method, 107
lookups, joining with, 90–91

M

Max method, 107, 108
Min method, 107, 108
mixed syntax queries, 14

MoveNext, 11
multiple generators, 74
multiple keys, joining, 86

N

namespaces (XML), 141
NextNode method, 127
Nodes method, 123
NodesAfterSelf method, 127
NodesBeforeSelf method, 127
non-equi join, 78
nullable type, casting to, 134
NullReferenceException, 125,
    135, 149

O

object hierarchies (projecting
    into), 68
object initializers, 30
ObjectTrackingEnabled, 43
OfType method, 101–103
OrderBy method, 4, 92–95, 97
  comprehension queries, 12
  lambda expressions, 7
OrderByDescending
    method, 92, 93
ordering, 92–95
  comparers and collations, 94
  IOrderedEnumerable, 94
  IOrderedQueryable, 94
  OrderBy method, 92–95
  OrderByDescending
      method, 92, 93
  Reverse method, 92
  ThenBy method, 92
  ThenByDescending
      method, 92, 93
outer iteration variables, 75–76
outer joins with
    GroupJoin, 88–90
outer joins with SelectMany
    method, 80–82

outer sequence
   join operators, 85
outer variable semantics, 17

P

Parent method, 126
Parse method, 117
predicate, 6
prefixes (XML), 141
PreviousNode method, 127
primary keys (LINQ to SQL), 41
progressively constructing
      queries, 5
projecting, 66–82
   comprehension syntax, 76–77
   concrete types, 71
   indexed projection, 68
   LINQ to SQL
      SelectMany method, 78–80
   outer iteration
      variables, 75–76
   outer joins with SelectMany
      method, 80–82
   Select (see Select method)
   SelectMany (see SelectMany
      method)
   subqueries and joins in LINQ
      to SQL, 69–71
   subqueries and object
      hierarchies, 68
projection strategies, 30–32

Q

quantifiers, 10, 111–112
   All method, 111
   Any method, 111
   Contains method, 111
   SequenceEqual method, 111
queries, 2
   building (see building query
      expressions)

constructing progressively, 5
interpreted (see interpreted
      queries)
local (see local queries)
mixed syntax, 14
operators (see query
      operators)
subqueries (see subqueries)
wrapping, 28–29
query comprehension syntax, 4,
      10
   (see also comprehension
      queries)
query continuation, 27, 88, 98
query operators, 2, 59–61
   categories, 59
   chaining, 4–6
   lambda expressions, 3, 7
   standard, 4
query processing, moving from
      database server to
      client, 40
query syntax (see comprehension
      queries)
Queryable class, 2, 33
   standard set of methods, 38

R

Range method, 113
range variable (see iteration
      variable)
refreshing objects (LINQ to
      SQL), 43
Remove method, 128, 130
   calling on sequence of
      nodes, 131
RemoveAll method, 129
RemoveAttributes method, 129
RemoveNodes method, 129
Repeat method, 113
Replace method, 128
ReplaceAll method, 129

ReplaceAttributes method, 129
ReplaceNodes method, 129
ReplaceWith method, 130
Reverse method, 9, 92

S

Save method, 118
Select method, 4, 11, 66, 84
    comprehension queries, 12
    concrete types, 71
    indexed projection, 68
    lambda expressions, 7
    LINQ to SQL, 69–71
    ordering, 9
    subqueries and object
        hierarchies, 68
SelectMany method, 66, 72–82,
        84
    comprehension syntax, 76–77
    joining, 77
    LINQ to SQL, 78–80
    outer iteration
        variables, 75–76
    outer joins, 80
    overview, 73–75
    versus Join, 85
SequenceEqual method, 111
sequences, 1
set operators, 100–101
    Concat method, 100
    Except method, 100
    Intersect method, 100
    Union method, 100
SetAttributeValue method, 129
SetElementValue method, 128,
        129
SetValue method, 128, 133
Single method, 9, 42, 104, 105
SingleOrDefault method, 104,
        105
Skip method, 9, 62, 65

SkipWhile method, 62, 66
SQL
    AVG (), 107
    COUNT( ), 107
    CROSS JOIN, 66
    EXCEPT, 100
    GROUP BY, 95
    INNER JOIN, 66, 82
    LEFT OUTER JOIN, 66, 82
    MAX( ), 107
    MIN( ), 107
    NOT IN, 62
    ORDER BY, 92, 104
    ORDER BY ... DESC, 104
    SELECT, 66
    SELECT DISTINCT, 62
    SELECT TOP 1, 104
    subqueries, 13
    SUM( ), 107
    UNION, 100
    UNION ALL, 100
    WHERE, 62, 111
    WHERE ... IN, 100, 111
    WHERE ROW_
        NUMBER, 62
    (see also LINQ to SQL)
SQL Server, 2, 34, 38, 39
    auto-incrementing field, 51
    ROW_NUMBER function, 65
SQL syntax versus LINQ query
        syntax, 13
SqlMetal, 45, 51
standard query operators, 59
subqueries, 22–25
    correlated, 24, 69
    deferred execution of, 25
    LINQ to SQL, 69–71
    Select method, 68
subsequences, expanding and
        flattening, 76
Sum method, 107, 109

System.Core, 1
System.Linq, 1
  standard query operators, 2
System.Linq.Expressions, 56

T

Table attribute, 40
Take method, 9, 62, 65
TakeWhile method, 62, 66
TextWriter, 118
ThenBy method, 92
ThenByDescending method, 92, 93
ToArray method, 40, 101, 103
ToDictionary method, 101, 103
ToList method, 40, 101, 103
ToLookup method, 101, 103
ToString method, 118, 121

U

Union method, 10, 100
updates, LINQ to SQL, 50
using System.Linq directive, 12

V

var keyword, 3, 31
Visual Studio, 45, 51

W

Where method, 2, 3, 4, 62–65
  comprehension queries, 12
  indexed filtering, 64
  lambda expressions, 6
  LINQ to SQL, 64
  ordering, 9
wrapping queries, 28–29

X

XAttribute, 116
  casting to nullable type, 134
  constructing, 118
  Remove method, 130
  SetValue method, 128
  Value property, 133–136
    getting values, 133–135
    setting values, 133
XComment, 116, 120
XContainer, 122
  Add method, 129
  AddFirst method, 129
  child nodes, 116
  decisions, 120
  Descendants method, 122
  Element method, 122
  Elements method, 122
  RemoveNodes method, 129
  ReplaceNodes method, 129
  ToString, 121
XDeclaration, 136, 137
  absence, 139
  XNode, 138
XDocument, 136–138
  accepted content, 136
  constructs, 137
  Root property, 138
  XElement, 137
XDocumentType, 137
X-DOM (see LINQ to XML)
XElement
  AncestorsAndSelf
      method, 126
  Attribute method, 128
  Attributes method, 128
  casting to nullable type, 134
  constructing, 118, 143

DescendantsAndSelf
method, 122
FirstAttribute method, 128
HasAttributes method, 128
HasElements method, 122
LastAttribute method, 128
Load method, 117
namespaces, 143
Parse method, 117
RemoveAll method, 129
RemoveAttributes
method, 129
ReplaceAll method, 129
ReplaceAttributes
method, 129
SetAttributeValue
method, 129
SetElementValue method, 129
SetValue method, 128
Value property, 133–136
getting values, 133–135
setting values, 133
XDocument, 137
XML
declarations, 139–140
names and
namespaces, 140–147
default
namespaces, 143–145
prefixes, 145–147
specifying namespaces in X-
DOM, 142–143
serialization, 139
(see also LINQ to XML)
XmlWriter, 118
XName, 142, 143
+ operator, 143
XNamespace, 142
XNode, 116, 122, 138

AddAfterSelf method, 130
AddBeforeSelf method, 130
Ancestors method, 126
child nodes, 116
ElementsAfterSelf
method, 127
ElementsBeforeSelf
method, 127
IsAfter method, 127
IsBefore method, 127
NextNode method, 127
NodesAfterSelf method, 127
NodesBeforeSelf method, 127
Parent method, 126
PreviousNode method, 127
Remove method, 130
ReplaceWith method, 130
XObject, 116
Document property, 138
XProcessingInstruction, 137
XStreamingElement, 151
XText
automatic concatenation, 136
values and mixed content
nodes, 135

Y

yield return, 19

By the same authors:

Table of Contents:

Introducing C#
C# Language Basics
Creating Types in C#
Advanced C# Features
Framework Fundamentals
Collections
LINQ Queries
LINQ Operators
LINQ to XML
Other XML Technologies
Disposal & Garbage Collection
Streams and I/O
Networking
Serialization
Assemblies
Reflection & Metadata
Threading
Asynchronous Methods
Application Domains
Integrating with Native DLLs
Diagnostics
Regular Expressions

www.albahari.com/nutshell